973   Mead, Robin.
MEA   Facts America: The Fifty States

DATE DUE

FACTS AMERICA

THE FIFTY
STATES

ROBIN & POLLY MEAD AND GARY A. LEWIS

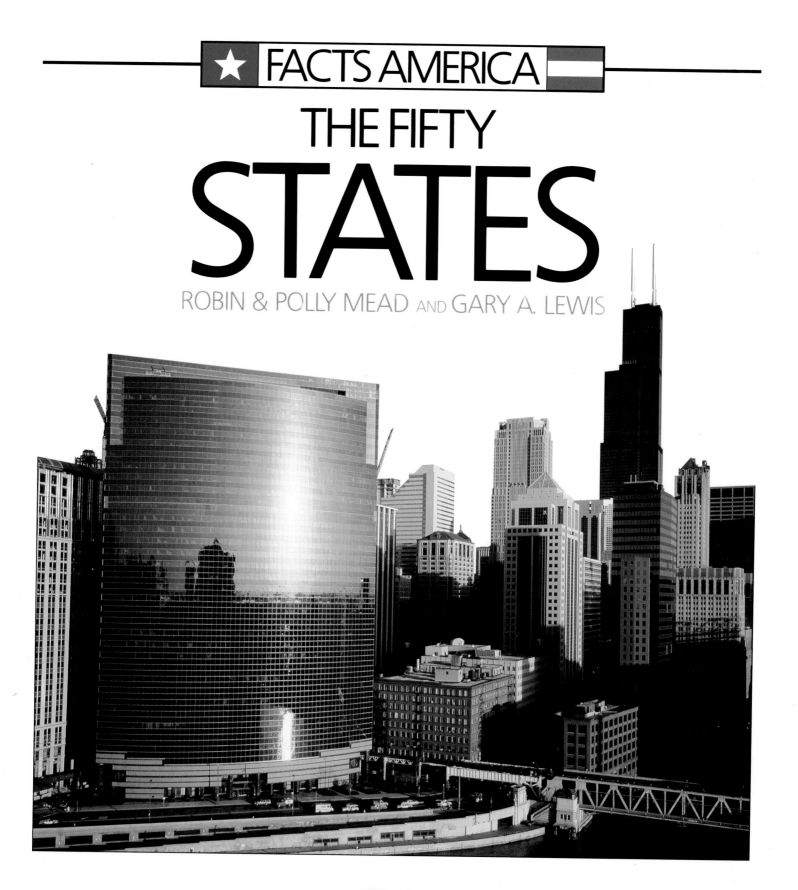

SMITHMARK

About the authors

Robin Mead is an author and journalist whose work appears in newspapers and magazines around the world. An avid traveler, Mr. Mead has written numerous books and travel guides. His wife, Polly Mead, trained as a teacher and worked in the travel industry before joining her husband as full-time co-writer, researcher, and "organizer in chief."

Gary A. Lewis is a children's author who has written more than 50 books and television scripts. Mr. Lewis received a graduate degree in English literature from Columbia University. He lives with his wife and two children in New York City.

Editor:
Philip de Ste. Croix

Designer:
Stonecastle Graphics Ltd

Picture research:
Leora Kahn

Coordinating editors:
Andrew Preston
Kristen Schilo

Production:
Ruth Arthur
Sally Connolly
Neil Randles
Andrew Whitelaw

Production editor:
Didi Charney

Director of production:
Gerald Hughes

Typesetter:
Pagesetters Incorporated

Color and monochrome reproduction:
Advance Laser Graphic Arts, Hong Kong

Printed and bound in Hong Kong
by Leefung-Asco Printers Ltd

1992 Colour Library Books Ltd
Godalming Business Centre
Woolsack Way, Godalming
Surrey GU7 1XW, United Kingdom
CLB 2610

This edition published in 1992 by
SMITHMARK Publishers Inc.
112 Madison Avenue
New York, NY 10016 USA

SMITHMARK books are available for bulk
purchase for sales promotion and premium
use. For details, write or call the manager
of special sales, SMITHMARK Publishers
Inc., 112 Madison Avenue, New York, NY 10016;
(212) 532-6600.

Library of Congress Cataloging-in-Publication Data

Mead, Robin.
    Facts America. The fifty states / Robin & Polly Mead & Gary A.
Lewis.
        p.   cm.
    Includes bibliographical references and index.
    Summary: Discusses the geography, cities, agriculture, and people
that make up the fifty states.
    ISBN 0-8317-2317-3 (hardcover)
    1. United States—Miscellanea—Juvenile literature. [1. United
States.]   I. Mead, Polly, 1946–   II. Lewis, Gary A., 1950–
III. Title.   IV. Title: Fifty states.
E156.M423   1992
973—dc20   92-9404

A beautiful view of Washington, D.C., at night. In the foreground is the Jefferson Memorial, a building that contains a 19-foot-high statue of Thomas Jefferson, the third president of the United States. In the background, we can see the dome of the nation's Capitol on Capitol Hill.

A note about this book

The contents of this book have been divided into five regional sections, as the accompanying map shows. Each region generally contains a set of ten states, which are grouped together because of their geographic proximity. While some readers may find these divisions a little unfamiliar at first, we hope that they will benefit from the book's symmetrical and balanced structure, which allows a similar number of states to be considered in each of the sections. For instance, the section entitled "The Northeast" includes New England and the Middle Atlantic states. Arkansas, Kentucky, and Tennessee, which are usually included in the South, are here grouped in "The Midwest and the Heartland." Similarly, Minnesota, which is more often included in the Midwest, is here grouped with "The West."

Each section opens with a detailed map of the group of states under consideration, so that the game plan of the book should soon become familiar to readers as the pattern unfolds.

Contents

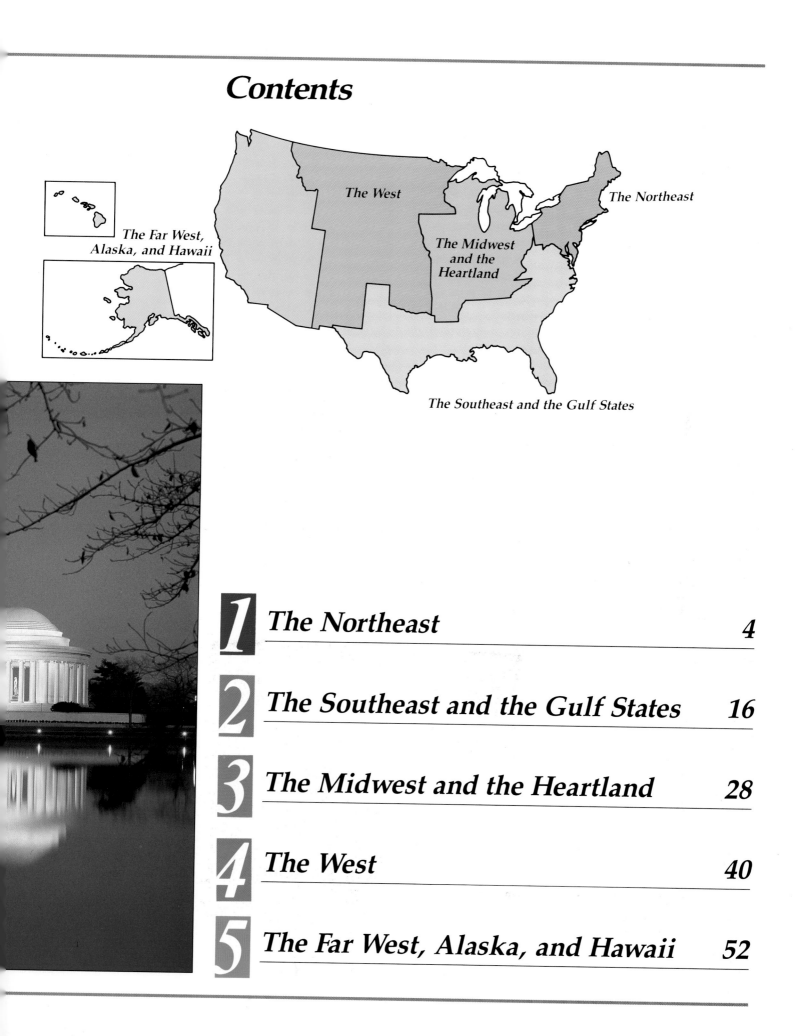

The Far West, Alaska, and Hawaii

The West

The Northeast

The Midwest and the Heartland

The Southeast and the Gulf States

1 The Northeast

Native Americans have lived in the United States for about 25,000 years. But what we often think of as "modern" America—the America of European and other immigrants—began in the northeast corner of the United States only a little over 300 years ago.

It might have started earlier. The Vikings probably landed here around 1000 A.D.; but no settlers followed. Christopher Columbus didn't reach these shores . . . he ended up farther south, in the Caribbean. And although the Dutch had colonized New York by the mid-1600s, it was the Pilgrim Fathers who began the wave of English immigration to the area that determined its future character. After they landed in Plymouth, Massachusetts, in 1620, the New World was truly born.

America's independence from British rule was born in the Northeast, too. In 1773, in Boston, Massachusetts, angry citizens dumped boxes of tea into the harbor to protest British taxation. Their action became known as the Boston Tea Party. The first shots of the revolutionary war were fired at Lexington and Concord, Massachusetts, in 1775. And the Declaration of Independence was signed in Philadelphia, Pennsylvania, on July 4, 1776, as the Liberty Bell rang.

CONNECTICUT (population 3.3 million in 5,018 sq mi)
Climate: moderate, but with snowy winters
State flower: mountain laurel
State bird: American robin
Capital: Hartford
Industries: manufacturing, fishing, agriculture, aerospace products, insurance
Entered Union: January 9, 1788

DELAWARE (population 0.7 million in 2,045 sq mi)
Climate: humid; hot summers, mild winters
State flower: peach blossom
State bird: blue hen chicken
Capital: Dover
Industries: chemistry, agriculture, fishing, manufacturing, food processing, transportation equipment
Entered Union: December 7, 1787

MAINE (population 1.2 million in 33,265 sq mi)
Climate: mild summers; cold, snowy winters
State flower: white pine cone and tassel
State bird: chickadee
Capital: Augusta
Industries: fishing, shipbuilding, forestry, textiles, insurance
Entered Union: March 15, 1820

MARYLAND (population 4.8 million in 10,460 sq mi)
Climate: humid; hot summers, generally mild winters
State flower: black-eyed Susan
State bird: Baltimore oriole
Capital: Annapolis
Industries: manufacturing, tourism, research, agriculture, fishing
Entered Union: April 28, 1788

MASSACHUSETTS (population 6 million in 8,284 sq mi)
Climate: mild summers, cold winters; colder in the west
State flower: mayflower
State bird: chickadee
Capital: Boston
Industries: manufacturing, greenhouse produce, fruit, cattle, fishing
Entered Union: February 6, 1788

NEW HAMPSHIRE (population 1.1 million in 9,279 sq mi)
Climate: highly varied, due to mountains, ocean
State flower: purple lilac
State bird: purple finch
Capital: Concord
Industries: agriculture, fishing, manufacturing, mining
Entered Union: June 21, 1788

◀ *New York was called New Amsterdam by the Dutch settlers who colonized it. This is how it might have looked in 1660.*

▼ *The Rainbow Bridge, just below Niagara Falls. Niagara tumbles 180 feet into Lake Ontario at the American/Canadian border.*

NEW JERSEY (population 7.7 million in 7,787 sq mi)
Climate: mild; cool summers, relatively warm winters
State flower: purple violet
State bird: eastern goldfinch
Capital: Trenton
Industries: manufacturing, research, mining, fishing, pharmaceuticals
Entered Union: December 18, 1787

NEW YORK (population 17.9 million in 49,108 sq mi)
Climate: varied; can be hot and humid in summer, very cold in winter
State flower: rose
State bird: bluebird
Capital: Albany
Industries: agriculture, commerce, manufacturing, tourism, finance, communications
Entered Union: July 26, 1788

PENNSYLVANIA (population 11.9 million in 45,308 sq mi)
Climate: moist with cold winters; warm, pleasant summers
State flower: mountain laurel
State bird: ruffed grouse
Capital: Harrisburg
Industries: steel, travel, manufacturing, agriculture, health
Entered Union: December 12, 1787

RHODE ISLAND (population 1 million in 1,212 sq mi)
Climate: mild summers and winters
State flower: violet
State bird: Rhode Island red
Capital: Providence
Industries: manufacturing, metals, jewelry, fishing, textiles
Entered Union: May 29, 1790

VERMONT (population 0.56 million in 9,614 sq mi)
Climate: short, cool summers; long, cold winters
State flower: red clover
State bird: hermit thrush
Capital: Montpelier
Industries: manufacturing, tourism, maple syrup, lumber, agriculture
Entered Union: March 4, 1791

◀ *The Statue of Liberty stands proudly against a backdrop of the World Trade Center and the rest of the magnificent New York skyline.*

▼ *In the fall, northeasterners see red (and gold and brown) as maples, birches, and oaks turn a variety of brilliant colors.*

Historical Highlights

The Algonquian peoples who lived on the Northeast coast were hunters and farmers whose wigwams and longhouses dotted the landscape. They must have been surprised and a little overwhelmed by their new neighbors, who were determined to turn the Northeast into a version of the world they had left behind.

1000 Viking landfall on the coast of Maine

1498–99 The Cabot expedition explores coastal Maine

1524 Giovanni Verrazano sails into Narragansett Bay

1604 The French settle on the shores of the St. Croix River, Maine

1607 The English settle at Kennebec, Maine

1609 Samuel de Champlain claims Vermont for France, visits the New York region. Henry Hudson explores the Hudson river, Sandy Hook Bay (New Jersey), Delaware Bay

1610 Lord de la Warr, governor of Virginia, sails into Delaware Bay

1614 Adriaen Bloch claims Connecticut for the Dutch

1620 The Pilgrim Fathers land at Plymouth, Massachusetts. First permanent settlements in New Hampshire

1624 The Dutch establish Fort Orange (Albany), the first permanent European settlement

1625 The Dutch begin building New Amsterdam (New York)

1630 The Puritans found Boston

1631 William Claiborne establishes a trading post on Kent Island, Maryland

1632 King Charles II's charter grants proprietorship of Maryland to Lord Baltimore

1633 First English settlement in Connecticut (Windsor)

1636 Roger Williams founds Providence, Rhode Island. Founding of Harvard, the first college in the colonies, by the Puritans

1637 Connecticut militia defeats the Pequot Indians in the Pequot War

1638 New Haven founded by wealthy Puritans

1641 Massachusetts adopts the first code of law—the Body of Liberties

1647 The Rhode Island settlements unite under English charter

1649 Religious toleration act passed in Maryland

1654 Puritan William Claiborne seizes control of Maryland

1658 Lord Baltimore regains control of Maryland from rebellious Puritans

1662 New York State receives its charter from England

1663 The English grant Rhode Island its second charter

1664 The Dutch surrender New Amsterdam to England; the English take control of Pennsylvania and of Dutch territory on the Delaware River

1681 King Charles II's charter grants proprietorship of Pennsylvania to William Penn

1687 Connecticut's charter preserved by being hidden in an oak tree near Hartford, later known as the Charter Oak

1692 Fourteen women and six men executed for witchcraft in Salem, Massachusetts

1701 William Penn granted Charter of Privileges

1754 Resistance against British taxes in Massachusetts

1770 The British kill a number of colonists during a protest in Boston

1773 At the Boston Tea Party, 340 chests of tea are dumped in Boston harbor to protest taxes imposed by Britain

1774 The New York Tea Party. Rhode Island bans import of slaves

1775 Revolution begins at Lexington and Concord

1776 Congress approves Declaration of Independence

1777 General Burgoyne surrenders to General Gates at Saratoga

1787 Delaware becomes the first state of the Union. Second is Pennsylvania; third, New Jersey. Constitution of the United States of America is signed in Philadelphia

1788 Connecticut becomes the fifth state; Massachusetts, sixth; Maryland, seventh; New Hampshire, ninth; New York, eleventh

1789 George Washington is inaugurated first president in New York

1790 Rhode Island becomes the 13th state

1791 Vermont becomes 14th state. Maryland donates land to form Washington, D.C.

1795 The nation's first hard-surfaced road built between Philadelphia and Lancaster, Pennsylvania

1797 John Adams of Massachusetts elected president

1814 Francis Scott Key writes "The Star-Spangled Banner," which becomes America's national anthem, after watching the defenders of Fort McHenry resist British attacks

1820 Maine becomes a separate state, the 23rd

1823 President James Monroe outlines the Monroe Doctrine

1825 The Erie Canal is opened, allowing development of the northern part of New York State

1831 The first railroad links Albany and Schenectady. William Lloyd Garrison publishes an antislavery newspaper, *The Liberator*

1846 First baseball game held in Hoboken, New Jersey. The New York Nine defeat the New York Knickerbockers, 23–1

1861 Outbreak of the Civil War, in which more Americans die than in World War II

1862 Union forces drive back Confederates from Antietam Creek, near Sharpsburg, Maryland

1863 Union forces defeat Confederates under Robert E. Lee at Gettysburg, Pennsylvania. Lincoln delivers Gettysburg Address. Riots in New York against drafting into the Union army

▼ *First footsteps in the land of the free. In 1620, the Pilgrims land at Plymouth, Massachusetts, after their momentous transatlantic voyage.*

▲ *An unhappy moment in history as a girl is accused of the black art of witchcraft. Many men and women were burned as witches in Salem in the 1690s.*

▲ *Opening shots of the American Revolution. The battle of Lexington marked the beginning of the fight for independence from Britain.*

◀ *The Boston Tea Party in 1773 was a protest against British taxes. Tons of tea were dumped into the harbor in a daring raid.*

▲ *The Declaration of Independence is signed by congressional leaders in 1776, marking the birth of a new nation.*

◀ *Francis Scott Key watches the American flag flying proudly over Fort McHenry during a British bombardment in the War of 1812. This event inspired him to write "The Star-Spangled Banner."*

◀ *Bootleggers: Beware! Kegs of beer are smashed during the Prohibition era, from 1919 to 1933.*

1864 Confederate soldiers raid St. Albans, Vermont, in the most northerly land action of the war. Maryland abolishes slavery

1865 President Lincoln shot in Ford's Theater, Washington D.C., by John Wilkes Booth

1879 Edison invents electric light at Menlo Park, New Jersey

1886 Dedication of Auguste Bartholdi's *The Statue of Liberty Enlightening the World*, a gift to America from the people of France

1901 President McKinley assassinated in Buffalo by Leon Czolgosz

1919–33 Prohibition, the banning of alcoholic beverages throughout America, is resisted by Maryland. Crime waves and gang wars in major cities

1926 Robert Goddard launches first liquid-fuel rocket at Auburn, Massachusetts

1929 Wall Street stock market collapses on Black Tuesday

1931 Empire State Building formally opens in New York

1944 The International Monetary Conference is held at Bretton Woods, New Hampshire

1957 The first full-scale nuclear power plant opens in Shippingport, Pennsylvania

1959 The St. Lawrence Seaway is opened

1960 The New York State Thruway is opened

1961 John F. Kennedy of Massachusetts becomes president

1964 New York State hosts the World's Fair

1969 Newport Bridge opens, linking Rhode Island with the mainland

1976 Referendum in New Jersey approves gambling in Atlantic City

1979 Nuclear accident at Three Mile Island power plant in Pennsylvania

1986 Four days of festivities celebrate the Statue of Liberty's 100th birthday

Natural Wonders

There are many areas of great natural beauty in the Northeast, beginning with Maine. Glaciers covered most of North America during the last ice age. As they slowly retreated to the north, the glaciers naturally lingered longest in this most northern state. There, they carved out great lakes. As they melted, they also created many new rivers. Today, Maine remains much like the beautiful wilderness that the glaciers left behind. Ten percent of it is covered by lakes, and an amazing 80 percent is still forest.

The glaciers also gently smoothed the Appalachian Mountains, which run north to south from Maine down to the southeastern states. These little sisters of the mighty Rockies are one of the natural barriers that slowed the movement of settlers toward the West.

South of Maine, in New Hampshire and Vermont, the Appalachians are represented by the lovely White and Green mountain ranges. In Franconia Notch State Park, New Hampshire, the cable cars of the Cannon Mountain aerial tramway offer a spectacular view of the White Mountains. From there, you can see the great stone face of the Old Man of the Mountains—a dramatic profile believed to be 200 million years

▲ *Niagara's thundering falls, which Native Americans called "the voices of the gods," are now a tourist attraction.*

▼ *In contrast to Niagara, the waters of Lake Placid in the Adirondacks are usually peaceful.*

▲ *The brilliant fall foliage of New England's maple groves decorates a region also famous for its beautiful coastline and countryside.*

▲ *Fall colors in the Adirondacks, among the world's oldest mountains. This area is protected from development.*

▼ *One of the world's longest walks, the Appalachian Trail is well over 1,000 miles long. This scenic route winds down from Maine almost to Atlanta, Georgia.*

old. Farther south, in New York, the Appalachians are represented by the Adirondack Mountains. It was here, in Lake Placid, that the 1980 Olympic Winter Games were held.

Another special feature of the Northeast is its remarkable Atlantic coastline. The great harbors of Boston and New York and the magnificent shoreline of Acadia National Park, on the coast of Maine, are excellent examples of its variety and value.

Native American legends bring a touch of romance to many of the natural wonders in the Northeast. The beautiful Finger Lakes, at the heart of New York State's wine-growing region, are said to be the finger marks of the Great Spirit, left as he laid his hand on the area to bless it.

And, of course, the greatest natural Northeast wonder is Niagara. The larger Horseshoe Falls are actually in Canada; but the American Falls are higher, at 182 feet.

Flora and Fauna

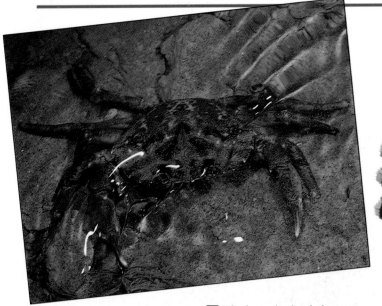

▼ Because it was a favorite food of the colonists, the wild turkey learned to roost in trees for safety. Here, a male bird displays his plumage.

▲ A shore crab. The ocean harvest, especially of oysters and lobsters, is important to the economy of the Northeast.

▼ The humpback whale was once hunted almost to extinction. Now it enjoys a measure of protection and thrives in the ocean off the northeastern coast.

The kindly, colorful landscape of the Northeast is still much as Nature intended it, despite our attempt to tame it. Oak leaves change from green to brown, birches are flooded with gold, and maple trees turn scarlet during the annual fall display. In fields and gardens, smaller trees like the lilac and a variety of bushes, shrubs, and other plants add their own colors to the rainbow at different times of the year.

Lively brown squirrels share the treetops with robins, bluebirds, finches, sparrows, and woodpeckers. Below them, shy deer, plump skunks, and bustling porcupines forage for food. In the forests, wild turkeys match the brilliance of the autumn leaves with their bright green, copper, and bronze feathers. And beavers work busily in their streams to dam the flow and build their watery empires.

But it is for its magnificent coastline that the Northeast is perhaps best known. Great whales cruise offshore while fishermen hunt bluefish and bass. And the shoreline offers its own harvest of lobsters, crabs, clams, and the famous Chesapeake Bay oysters.

Many breeds of domestic ▶ chickens have been bred in the United States. Perhaps the most famous is the Rhode Island red.

▲ *This large, brownish variety of woodpecker is called the common flicker. Flickers that live in the eastern United States have a red patch on their necks.*

▼ *These blue and yellow lupins bloom all summer long, adding lovely patches of color to the landscape.*

Yankee Ingenuity

America's oldest and most prestigious families can often trace their roots back to the first European settlers. But whether or not their ancestors "came over on the *Mayflower*," their children have made it into the history books.

William Penn (1644–1718) Penn converted to Quakerism in his 20s and was repeatedly jailed for his beliefs. In Europe, he met other Quakers eager to escape persecution and settle in the New World. In 1681, Penn and his followers founded Pennsylvania just west of the Delaware River.

Eli Whitney (1765–1825) Whitney was born in Westborough, Massachusetts. Moving to Georgia in 1793, he invented a machine that cleaned cotton 50 times faster than by hand. Later, he produced rifles for the government. He became known as the "father of mass production" because his rifles were the first to have standard, interchangeable parts.

Emily Dickinson (1830–1886) Born in Amherst, Massachusetts, Dickinson is one of the greatest American poets. Her work is known for its wit, delicacy, and directness. When a young woman, Dickinson became a recluse. For the rest of her life, although she corresponded with many friends, she saw almost no one. She published

▲ *John Fitzgerald Kennedy, America's most famous postwar president. He was elected in 1960 but assassinated in Dallas three years later.*

▼ *Known as the "father of mass production," Eli Whitney works on the cotton gin, the invention that made him famous.*

only seven poems during her lifetime. But after her death, her sister found over a thousand poems in her bureau.

Franklin Delano Roosevelt (1882–1945) America's only four-term president. Roosevelt led the United States out of the Great Depression and through most of World War II with the same determination with which he'd faced a severe case of polio that had left him paralyzed from the waist down. He died in his fourth presidential term, on April 12, 1945—less than a month before Germany surrendered to the Allies.

John F. Kennedy (1917–1963) Born in Brookline, Massachusetts, JFK was a Harvard graduate, war hero, and successful author and Pulitzer Prize winner for his book *Profiles in Courage.* Kennedy was the first Catholic to be elected president. He served from 1960 until he was assassinated in Dallas on November 22, 1963.

Gone fishin.' Calvin Coolidge (1872–1933) was a quiet, sensible man from Plymouth Notch, Vermont, who became vice president in 1920 and president in 1923 when Warren G. Harding died.

Hiawatha (c. 1570) This Mohawk leader lived in what is now northern New York State. He helped found the Iroquois League, which ended war among the Iroquois tribes.

Robert Fulton (1765–1815) A native of Lancaster, Pennsylvania, Fulton is best known for designing and building the first commercially successful steamboat.

"Uncle Sam" Wilson (1766–1854) In 1812, Wilson, a butcher from Saratoga, New York, began stamping "U.S." on barrels of salt meat for the army—a symbol that locals claimed stood for "Uncle Sam."

Henry Wadsworth Longfellow (1807–82) Born in Portland, Maine, Longfellow was a popular American poet. He wrote "The Song of Hiawatha" and "Paul Revere's Ride."

Theodore Roosevelt (1858–1919) Born in New York City, Roosevelt became president in 1900 when William McKinley was assassinated.

William Edward Burghardt Du Bois (1868–1963) Born in Great Barrington, Massachusetts, Du Bois cofounded the National Association for the Advancement of Colored People (NAACP).

Thurgood Marshall (1908–   ) From Baltimore, Maryland, he became the first black justice to sit on the Supreme Court when appointed by President Lyndon B. Johnson in 1967.

▲ *Louisa May Alcott (1832–88) was born in Germantown, Pennsylvania. Her most famous book,* Little Women, *was published in 1868.*

Born in Brooklyn, "Scarface" ▶ *Al Capone (1899–1947) became a famous gang leader in Chicago during the 1920s. He was blamed for the St. Valentine's Day Massacre of 1929 but was convicted only of tax evasion.*

▲ *The New York Yankees baseball star Babe Ruth (1895–1948), a native of Baltimore, was one of the most famous athletes ever.*

The son of Russian ▶ *immigrants, the great composer Aaron Copland (1900–1990) was born in New York. He used traditional folk tunes in works such as* Billy the Kid *and* Appalachian Spring.

The Great Cities

Washington, D.C., is not just the capital of the United States. It is also one of the most beautiful cities in the world. It was designed by French engineer Pierre Charles L'Enfant to resemble Paris, with its wide avenues, beautiful squares, and sweeping views. The site was chosen by George Washington because it was near his Mount Vernon home. But John Adams was the first president to actually move in, in 1800.

The 555-foot Washington Monument and the gleaming Capitol Building, whose cast-iron dome was designed to look like marble, are the most famous Washington landmarks. According to law, no building in the city can be taller than these two. The Lincoln Memorial and the White House are two of Washington's other great buildings. The city is noted for its art galleries and museums, including the National Gallery of Art and the Smithsonian. It is also home to the Library of Congress.

Baltimore Founded in 1724 as a trading center, Baltimore, Maryland, has always been a business and financial center. It was at Fort McHenry, Baltimore, that the star-spangled banner flew. Francis Scott Key's manuscript of the national anthem can be seen at the Maryland Historical Society's city headquarters.

▲ *The Washington Monument towers over the Capitol's dome and the Lincoln Memorial.*

The skyline of Boston, the ▶ *city where modern America was born*

14

◀ *The star-spangled banner flies proudly from the stern of a yacht on the harbor at Baltimore, where the national anthem was written.*

▲ *The world's most famous skyline is that of New York. The Empire State and Chrysler buildings soar above more recent constructions.*

▲ *A panoramic view of Philadelphia's Independence Hall and Independence Square*

Boston The capital of Massachusetts, Boston is the oldest city in America (1630); nearby, in Cambridge, is the oldest college (Harvard). Boston's 1.5-mile Freedom Trail winds past many historic sites, including Paul Revere's house and the Old North Church, where "one if by land, two if by sea" lanterns were hung to alert the colonists to a British attack. The trail ends at the spot where the USS *Constitution*, "Old Ironsides," is moored.

New York The Big Apple is the brash, noisy, crowded business heart of America. The country's largest city, it has a magnificent skyline and a vital cultural life. The Statue of Liberty guards its harbor, and Ellis Island continues to welcome millions of immigrants to its shores. The Metropolitan Museum of Art and the Museum of Modern Art are full of treasures, and other museums and art galleries abound.

Philadelphia One of the birthplaces of American independence, Philadelphia, Pennsylvania, is built around Independence Square, now restored to its 18th-century elegance and designated a National Historical Park. The Liberty Bell, which was rung to celebrate the signing of the Declaration of Independence, is preserved here.

2 The Southeast and the Gulf States

Long before the Pilgrims landed in Massachusetts, Spanish ships roamed the seas around South Carolina and Florida. By 1650, there were 300,000 European settlers living in what is now South Carolina. They soon began to displace the Native American populations. Many Native Americans were killed by European diseases. Others were pushed aside as European settlements expanded. And in 1830, nearly all who remained were deported to Indian Territory (Oklahoma).

The Southeast provided its new settlers with fairly comfortable lives. Rich farmlands reached from the Virginias to the Mississippi basin. King Cotton flourished here—and slavery was introduced to the New World here. Minerals, including gold, were also plentiful. Farther west, the land was more hostile. But there were cattle . . . and there was oil.

Today, cotton shares the old plantation lands with sugar cane. But the genteel courtesies of a bygone age are still commonplace. What is also commonplace in the Southeast is the sun. Florida, in particular, attracts more and more tourists each year from both America and Europe. And tourists are not the only ones who like clear skies. Astronauts like them, too. That is why Florida has become the center of the U.S. space program.

ALABAMA (population 4 million in 51,705 sq mi)
Climate: mild winters and hot summers
State flower: camellia
State bird: yellowhammer
Capital: Montgomery
Industries: agriculture, chemicals, electronics, manufacturing, paper, apparel
Entered Union: December 14, 1819

NORTH CAROLINA (population 6.6 million in 52,669 sq mi)
Climate: hot in the southeast, mild in the western mountains
State flower: dogwood
State bird: cardinal
Capital: Raleigh
Industries: agriculture (especially tobacco), manufacturing, tourism
Entered Union: November 21, 1789

SOUTH CAROLINA (population 3.5 million in 31,113 sq mi)
Climate: warm throughout the year
State flower: yellow jessamine
State bird: Carolina wren
Capital: Columbia
Industries: manufacturing, textiles, agriculture, timber, chemical products, tourism
Entered Union: May 23, 1788

FLORIDA (population 12.9 million in 58,664 sq mi)
Climate: tropical in the south, warm and rainy in the north
State flower: orange blossom
State bird: mockingbird
Capital: Tallahassee
Industries: agriculture (especially citrus fruit), tourism, manufacturing, electronics, printing
Entered Union: March 3, 1845

GEORGIA (population 6.4 million in 58,910 sq mi)
Climate: warm, humid summers; short, mild winters
State flower: Cherokee rose
State bird: brown thrasher
Capital: Atlanta
Industries: agriculture, tourism, manufacturing, forestry, chemical products
Entered Union: January 2, 1788

LOUISIANA (population 4.2 million in 47,752 sq mi)
Climate: mild and wet, with hot summers
State flower: magnolia
State bird: eastern brown pelican
Capital: Baton Rouge
Industries: agriculture, manufacturing, construction, transportation, mining, chemicals, electronics
Entered Union: April 30, 1812

▲ The "discovery" of Mississippi. In about 1540, the Spanish explorer Hernando de Soto marches westward in search of treasure.

The Everglades are not the ▶ only large swamp area in the Southeast. This is the Okefenokee Swamp, in Georgia, where alligators thrive.

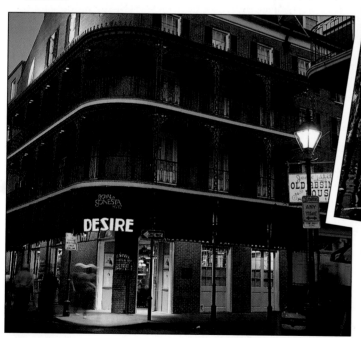

▲ In the Vieux Carré, or French Quarter, of modern New Orleans, Louisiana, an oyster bar beckons customers to enjoy its seafood.

The railroad brought sun ▶ seekers to Florida, where Miami and Miami Beach have now grown into one of the world's top tourist destinations.

MISSISSIPPI (population 2.6 million in 47,689 sq mi)
Climate: warm and moist, with long summers, short winters
State flower: magnolia
State bird: mockingbird
Capital: Jackson
Industries: agriculture, shipping, manufacturing, timber, seafood
Entered Union: December 10, 1817

TEXAS (population 17 million in 266,807 sq mi)
Climate: extremely varied, wet in the northeast
State flower: bluebonnet
State bird: mockingbird
Capital: Austin
Industries: manufacturing, oil, cattle, aerospace, electrical machinery, cotton
Entered Union: December 29, 1845

VIRGINIA (population 6.1 million in 40,767 sq mi)
Climate: mild, seldom below freezing
State flower: dogwood
State bird: cardinal
Capital: Richmond
Industries: agriculture, manufacturing, technology, research, tourism
Entered Union: June 25, 1788

WEST VIRGINIA (population 1.8 million in 24,232 sq mi)
Climate: warm summers, moderately cold winters
State flower: big rhododendron
State bird: cardinal
Capital: Charleston
Industries: manufacturing, agriculture, mining, tourism
Entered Union: June 20, 1863

Historical Highlights

While American communities were developing in the Northeast, the Southeast and the area around the Gulf of Mexico played host to struggles among the powers of Europe. The Spanish, the French, and the British all came. Some of them conquered, staying on to tame and civilize this new land, and to create the cosmopolitan nature of the region. Rich in natural resources and now rich in human resources, too, the Southeast and the Gulf states developed and flourished.

1492 Christopher Columbus lands on islands in the Caribbean

1513 de Pineda of Spain sails into Mobile Bay and maps coast of Texas

1539–42 Hernando de Soto of Spain explores Florida, Alabama, Mississippi, Georgia, and northeast Texas

1559 The Spaniard Tristan de Luna establishes a settlement in Alabama

1565 Pedro Menendez de Avile of Spain founds St. Augustine, Florida

1584 Sir Walter Raleigh's expedition lands on the coastline of Virginia

1585 The first English colony in America is founded at Roanoke Island

1607 The Virginia Company of London establishes the colony of Jamestown, Virginia

1612 John Rolfe saves the Virginia colony by introducing tobacco growing and exporting

1614 John Rolfe marries Indian bride, Pocahontas

1619 In Virginia, the first representative legislature meets in Jamestown (the House of Burgesses), and the Dutch bring in the first slaves

1629 King Charles II grants Virginia's charter to governor Sir Robert Heath

1682 Robert Cavelier reaches the mouth of the Mississippi River and claims the area for France; Spanish missionaries build two missions near El Paso, Texas

1693 The College of William and Mary is founded in Williamsburg, Virginia

1699 Le Moyne establishes the first French colony at Old Biloxi, Mississippi. Louisiana becomes a royal French colony

1718 Governor Bienville founds New Orleans; the Spanish build a mission near San Antonio, Texas

1726 Morgan Morgan, the first permanent European settler, builds a cabin at Bunker Hill, West Virginia

1727 Germans arrive from Pennsylvania and found New Mecklenburg (now Shepherdstown, West Virginia)

1733 The English, led by James Edward Oglethorpe, first settle Georgia

1754–55 General Braddock is defeated in the French and Indian Wars

1762 France cedes Louisiana to Spain

1763 Spain cedes Florida to England; Mississippi becomes English after the French and Indian Wars

1775 George Washington becomes commander of the Continental army

1776 In Virginia, a committee headed by Thomas Jefferson drafts the Declaration of Independence

1780 The battle of King's Mountain, a turning point of the Revolution, is fought in North Carolina

1781 Lord Cornwallis surrenders at Yorktown, Virginia, the last major battle of the Revolution

1788 Georgia becomes the fourth state; South Carolina, the eighth; Virginia, the tenth

1789 George Washington inaugurated first president; North Carolina becomes the 12th state

1793 France gives Alabama to England. Eli Whitney invents the cotton gin

1800 Spain cedes Louisiana to France

1803 The United States gains much territory under the Louisiana Purchase agreement with France. The land is acquired for $15 million

1812 Louisiana becomes the 18th state

1813 The United States captures Mobile Bay from the Spanish

1814 After battle of Horseshoe Bend, Creek tribe surrenders its lands, equaling half the state of Alabama, to the United States

1815 Andrew Jackson's forces beat the British at battle of New Orleans

1817 Mississippi becomes the 20th state. Alabama Territory is created when Mississippi Territory is split into two

1819 Alabama becomes the 22nd state

▼ *A touching moment in the history of Virginia is captured in an early engraving. Pocahontas saves Captain John Smith from execution by members of the Powhatan tribe in 1607.*

◀ *This painting by De Land shows Thomas Jefferson reading the draft of the Declaration of Independence to Benjamin Franklin. It was adopted by the Continental Congress in 1776.*

▲ *The siege of the Alamo, in 1836. The garrison of 187 was wiped out by the Mexican army in the course of a ferocious battle.*

◀ *The end of the Civil War. The South's General Robert E. Lee surrenders to Union General Ulysses S. Grant at Appomattox in 1865.*

1821 The United States gains control of Florida. Texas is part of the new empire of Mexico

1822 Congress establishes the Florida Territory

1835 Seminole wars in Florida give rise to massacres on both sides. Texas revolts against Mexico

1836 Texas gains independence from Mexico after the fall of the Alamo and Sam Houston's subsequent defeat of the Mexicans at San Jacinto

1845 Florida becomes the 27th state; Texas becomes the 28th

1859 John Brown raids the federal arsenal at Harpers Ferry

1861 Civil War begins with the Confederates firing on Fort Sumter

1862 Union naval forces capture New Orleans

1863 West Virginia becomes the 35th state. Confederate troops defeat Union forces at Chickamauga, Georgia; Union troops capture Vicksburg after a long siege. Stonewall Jackson dies from wounds received at the battle of Chancellorsville

1864 General Sherman captures Atlanta and marches to the sea

1865 General Johnston's surrender to Sherman near Durham Station, North Carolina, 17 days after Lee's surrender to Grant, marks the virtual end of the Civil War

1868 Alabama, North Carolina, Florida, and Louisiana rejoin the Union

1870 Virginia, Georgia, Mississippi, and Texas are readmitted to the Union

1903 The Wright brothers make the first motor-driven flight at Kitty Hawk, North Carolina

1906 Start of the Everglades drainage program at Fort Lauderdale

1925 Texas is the first state to have a woman governor, Mrs. Miriam Ferguson

1928 Huey Long is elected governor of Louisiana. He serves as governor, then senator, until his assassination in 1935

1938 The Overseas Highway in Florida is opened

1956 The town of Montgomery, Alabama, is ordered to desegregate its buses

1958 First U.S. satellite is launched into space from Cape Canaveral, Florida

1961 First U.S. manned space flight by Commander Alan Shepard from Cape Canaveral

1963 President Kennedy is assassinated in Dallas

1965 Martin Luther King, Jr., marches in Alabama to protest against electoral discrimination

1969 The crew members of *Apollo 11*, the first men on the moon, are launched from the Kennedy Space Center, Florida

1973 A major southern city elects a black mayor, Maynard Jackson, in Atlanta

1981 First flight of space shuttle *Columbia* from Kennedy Space Center, Florida

▲ *A painting of aviator Wilbur Wright with his airplane in France during a visit to Europe at the beginning of this century*

◀ *Astronaut Edwin Aldrin walks on the lunar surface during the successful* Apollo 11 *mission in July 1969.*

Natural Wonders

It may look like green ▶ pastureland, but this saw grass "prairie" is actually a marsh in Florida's Everglades. The only safe way to travel around here is by skimming over land and water in a fan-driven airboat.

▼ Colorful water lilies decorate the waters of the Okefenokee Swamp in Georgia. This natural wilderness is formed by the headwaters of the Suwannee River.

The Southeast contains some of America's loveliest natural wonders. They include the sulfur springs and Bluestone Gorge of West Virginia, the swamplands of Georgia, Florida, and Louisiana, the mighty Mississippi River, and the plains of Texas.

One of the most popular regions is Virginia's Blue Ridge Mountains and the Alleghenies—the site of the 90-foot Natural Bridge that the Native Americans called "the bridge of God," which soars 215 feet above Cedar Creek. Others include the Cumberland Gap, a natural gateway in the Alleghenies; the Great Smoky Mountains of North Carolina and Tennessee; the Okefenokee Swamp, a wilderness area in Georgia and Florida; and the Palo Duro Canyon, which was carved out of the Texas landscape by river waters 90 million years ago.

But perhaps the best known of the Southeast's wonders are the junglelike swamplands to the south, especially Florida's Everglades. The Everglades covers a large area of central Florida. At its highest point, it is only a few feet higher than sea level. The Everglades contains a wide variety of animals, including alligators, and makes up one of the largest national parks in America.

▲ A spectacular look at the Blue Ridge Mountains. This view, toward Whiteside and Looking Glass Rock, is from the parkway.

▲ Another view of the Blue Ridge Mountains, in North Carolina. If you have ever wondered why the mountains got their name, this evening view of them provides the answer.

◄ An aerial view of the Everglades in winter, showing grassy knolls and islets surrounded by waterways. A local tribe of Native Americans still lives on the islets, making its living from tourism and "farming" alligators.

Flora and Fauna

Cotton was once the main crop of the Southeast. It is still important, but these days, you are just as likely to see sugar cane growing in the fields. The region also supports a huge variety of wildlife. There are the usual residents of North America—deer, skunks, raccoons, and bobcats. But they have some unusual neighbors here, include scaly coated armadillos, savage wild boars and cougars, cute flying squirrels, alligators, loggerhead turtles, pelicans, and rare Everglades kites. Other rare birds that live in the Southeast include the greater snow goose and the black-throated and cerulean warblers.

Offshore, fishermen chase tuna and marlin, while golden centennial trout and black crappie swim in the rivers and swamplands. The swamplands are also home to many kinds of ferns, as well as to the insect-eating Venus's fly-trap plant, which also flourishes in Alabama. Camellias grow in the coastal regions, and Spanish moss reminds us that we are in the Deep South.

▼ *Red, white, pink, or spotted flowers provide the bursts of brilliant color that decorate camellia bushes throughout the coastal areas. A garden favorite, too, they blossom in winter or early spring.*

Feathered fisherman of the ▶ Southeast, the pelican can have a wingspan of up to ten feet. Brown pelicans, like this one, dive to make their catches.

▼ *The toothy "smile" of this 500-pound alligator is misleading. At 18 feet long, with huge jaws and a nerve-racking roar, the adult alligator is a beast to avoid.*

▲ *Largest of the sea turtles, this loggerhead can grow to eight feet in length and weigh up to 1,500 pounds.*

An Everglades kite glides ▶ *over the swamp, searching for the water snails that are its only food. The kite, a rare form of hawk, scoops up the snails with its hooked bill.*

A glance at the names of the people the Southeast and the Gulf states have put in history books suggests that they have at least one trait in common. Having made up their minds to do something, they do it.

George Washington (1732–99) The "father of our country" was born in Westmoreland County, Virginia. He was a surveyor before joining the militia and serving heroically in the French and Indian Wars. Later, he led the battle for independence and helped to formulate the American Constitution in 1787. In 1789, he became America's first president.

Booker T. Washington (1856–1915) Born into slavery in Virginia, Washington became a respected educator and active spokesman for civil rights. He helped found Alabama's Tuskegee Institute—one of the leading black educational institutions in America.

George Washington Carver (c. 1864–1943) The son of slaves, Carver was one of America's leading agricultural chemists. He is best known for his experiments with soybeans and peanuts at Tuskegee Institute. He discovered many uses for

▼ *George Washington was elected America's first president in 1789. He had fought colonialism and helped draft the Constitution.*

A man with a dream— ▶ *Martin Luther King, Jr. America's most famous civil rights leader was the son of an Atlanta churchman.*

▲ *World War II hero, military leader, and postwar president, Dwight D. Eisenhower (1890–1969) was born in Texas. His popularity swept him to the presidency in the 1952 election, and he served two terms.*

them, including planting them to help replenish soil depleted from years of growing cotton.

Helen Keller (1880–1968) Born blind and deaf in Tuscumbia, Alabama, Keller was taught to communicate through touch and learned to speak and write. She then dedicated herself to working on behalf of the handicapped.

Martin Luther King, Jr. (1929–68) The son of a Baptist pastor in Atlanta, Georgia, King was ordained as a minister while in his teens. He led the nonviolent civil rights battle against segregation in the 1950s and 1960s. In 1964, he won the Nobel Peace Prize, but he was assassinated in Memphis four years later.

General Robert E. Lee ▶
*(1807–70) was the South's
greatest military leader during
the Civil War. An experienced
soldier from Virginia, he was
popular with his men.*

▼ *Thomas Jefferson (1743–1826),
from Virginia, was the
principal author of the
Declaration of Independence in
1776. He became president in
1801.*

Patrick Henry (1736–99) Born in Hanover County,
Virginia, Patrick Henry was a political leader during the
revolutionary war. He was a powerful orator and is famous
for the words "Give me liberty or give me death."

Hiram Revels (1822–1901) A professional educator born in
Fayetteville, North Carolina, Revels recruited for the Union
during the Civil War. He was the first black member of the
U.S. Senate, where he represented Mississippi as a
Republican.

Henry Flagler (1830–1913) Born in New York, Flagler made
his life in the South, where he developed Florida by
extending the railroad down the East Coast and building
hotels and resorts like Key West.

Marjorie Kinnan Rawlings (1896–1953) Although born in
Washington, D.C., Rawlings, a talented novelist, moved to
the backwoods of Florida in 1928. This is where most of her
work is set, including *Cross Creek*, an account of her life
there, and the Pulitzer Prize-winning *The Yearling*.

▼ *A New Orleans legend.
Trumpeter and bandleader
Louis Armstrong (1900–
1971) became one of
America's most famous
musicians.*

▲ *One of the greatest
boxers in history,
Alabama's Joe Louis
(1914–81) defended
the World
Heavyweight title
25 times.*

The Great Cities

Having risen from its ashes after being burned to the ground by General William Tecumseh Sherman during the Civil War, **Atlanta**, Georgia, has become a boomtown of flourishing businesses and excellent sports facilities. A top attraction is the nearby 32,000-acre Stone Mountain park, featuring huge carvings of Confederate heroes Jefferson Davis, Robert E. Lee, and Stonewall Jackson.

Charleston A settlement originally named in honor of England's King Charles II, modern Charleston, South Carolina, is a major seaport that still manages to retain its quaint streets, fine churches, historic homes, and colorful gardens. Harbor boat rides include a crossing to Fort Sumter, the Civil War landmark.

Dallas Cow town turned oil town, Dallas—with nearby Fort Worth—has become the booming business center of Texas, as well as the star of a long-running TV series. Its skyline is impressive, and some of the skyscrapers are tourist attractions in their own right.

▲ Beautiful Broad Street in historic Charleston, South Carolina, has fine churches, stylish homes, colorful gardens, and horse-drawn taxis!

Atlanta has grown from ▶ a sleepy southern town into a flourishing commercial center—and host city for the 1996 Olympic Summer Games.

◀ *The skyline of Dallas is eye-catching by day or night. Many buildings in this picture have been built on former railroad land.*

▲ *New Orleans is the most famous city on the banks of the mighty Mississippi River. Behind the river frontage is the lively French Quarter.*

▼ *Miami and the adjoining Miami Beach have become a top vacation playground because of Florida's mild climate.*

Miami The hub of Florida, Miami is actually a collection of municipalities. The most famous is Miami Beach—a narrow strip of land separated from the rest of Miami by Biscayne Bay. Miami is frequented by retired folk and holidaymakers from all over the world. It offers the top hotels, shops, and entertainment of Miami Beach, plus the atmospheric excitement of the Cuban-style Little Havana, located in Miami itself.

New Orleans The home of jazz and Creole cooking, New Orleans, Louisiana, boasts the famous Vieux Carré, or French Quarter. It attracts visitors from all over the world. Walking tours of the old part of the city are popular, past French-style buildings with flower-filled wrought-iron balconies and famous restaurants. In Preservation Hall, traditional jazz is still played. And there's street music in New Orleans practically around the clock.

3 The Midwest and the Heartland

The Midwest and the heartland provide many examples of the vast diversity of America. Great industries were founded in the north because of the mineral wealth of the land and the excellent transportation provided by the Great Lakes and the mighty Mississippi River. Chicago is one of the financial centers of the country. But toward the south, pockets of industry give way to the gentle farmlands of Illinois, the bluegrass of Kentucky, and the Great Smoky Mountains of Tennessee, where Clingmans Dome stands—the highest point east of the Mississippi.

The area is full of contradictions. Abraham Lincoln and Jefferson Davis—opposing leaders during the Civil War—were both born here, on Kentucky farms. And Michigan, although it is inland, actually has a longer coastline than any other state except Alaska—longer than the Atlantic coast from Maine to Florida!

But the spirit and dedication that motivated Abraham Lincoln—who for a time lived in Kentucky, Indiana, *and* Illinois—is reflected in the people of the Midwest and the heartland. This is perhaps what gives the region its distinct character.

ARKANSAS (population 2.4 million in 53,187 sq mi)
Climate: hot summers, mild winters, rainy
State flower: apple blossom
State bird: mockingbird
Capital: Little Rock
Industries: agriculture (especially cotton), mining, manufacturing, forestry, poultry, electrical goods
Entered Union: June 15, 1836

ILLINOIS (population 11.4 million in 56,345 sq mi)
Climate: cold winters, hot summers, very variable
State flower: native violet
State bird: cardinal
Capital: Springfield
Industries: agriculture, finance, insurance, manufacturing, printing, chemicals
Entered Union: December 3, 1818

INDIANA (population 5.5 million in 36,185 sq mi)
Climate: temperate climate, four distinct seasons
State flower: peony
State bird: cardinal
Capital: Indianapolis
Industries: manufacturing, agriculture, metals and machinery
Entered Union: December 11, 1816

IOWA (population 2.8 million in 56,275 sq mi)
Climate: long, snowy winters; short, hot summers
State flower: wild rose
State bird: eastern goldfinch
Capital: Des Moines
Industries: agriculture, manufacturing, insurance, meat packing and processing, farm machinery, fertilizers, automobile components
Entered Union: December 28, 1846

KENTUCKY (population 3.7 million in 40,410 sq mi)
Climate: warm summers, cool winters, rainy
State flower: goldenrod
State bird: cardinal
Capital: Frankfort
Industries: manufacturing (especially whiskey), textiles, coal mining, construction, agriculture (especially cattle, horses, tobacco)
Entered Union: June 1, 1792

MICHIGAN (population 9.3 million in 58,527 sq mi)
Climate: well-defined seasons, tempered by Great Lakes
State flower: apple blossom
State bird: robin
Capital: Lansing
Industries: manufacturing (especially automobiles), agriculture, mining
Entered Union: January 26, 1837

◀ *Frontiersmen defend themselves from a Native American ambush during an era that saw the opening up of the American heartland.*

▼ *The Great Lakes dominate the northern half of the Midwest. These rocky shores are those of Lake Superior.*

MISSOURI (population 5.1 million in 69,697 sq mi)
Climate: warm summers, moderate winters
State flower: hawthorn
State bird: bluebird
Capital: Jefferson City
Industries: manufacturing (especially chemicals), agriculture, food products, aerospace, electronics
Entered Union: August 10, 1821

OHIO (population 10.8 million in 41,330 sq mi)
Climate: temperate but variable, rainy
State flower: scarlet carnation
State bird: cardinal
Capital: Columbus
Industries: agriculture, livestock, manufacturing (especially machinery, metal products)
Entered Union: March 1, 1803

TENNESSEE (population 4.9 million in 42,144 sq mi)
Climate: humid, mild winters, warm summers
State flower: iris
State bird: mockingbird
Capital: Nashville
Industries: construction, transportation, electronics, communications, chemicals
Entered Union: June 1, 1796

WISCONSIN (population 4.9 million in 56,153 sq mi)
Climate: bitter winters; short, warm summers
State flower: wood violet
State bird: robin
Capital: Madison
Industries: agriculture, transportation, communications, manufacturing, paper and wood products, milk and cheese production
Entered Union: May 29, 1848

◀ *One of the greatest cities in the Midwest is Chicago, on the southern shores of Lake Michigan. The commercial hub of the region, its spectacular skyline is known around the world. This view, showing the Sears Tower (right), is from the John Hancock Building.*

Historical Highlights

"Go west, young man" was the cry of those young men who settled the United States in the late 18th and early 19th centuries. But many obstacles stood in their way—including the Native Americans who had ranged this land freely for so long.

It was in this heartland area that the battle for the nation's western civilization and culture was fought and won. Here are the highlights.

1540-41 Spaniard Hernando de Soto explores Tennessee and Arkansas

1620 Étienne Brulé, a French explorer, visits Michigan

1634 Wisconsin is "discovered" by Jean Nicolet of France

1668 Father Jacques Marquette of France founds the first settlement at Sault Saint Marie, Michigan, with Father Claude Dablon

1670 French explorer Robert Cavelier reaches Ohio

1673 Frenchmen Louis Joliet and Father Marquette are the first Europeans to set foot in and explore Iowa, Illinois, Missouri, Arkansas, and Tennessee. They travel by boat along the Mississippi River

1679 Cavelier reaches Indiana

1682 Cavelier claims the entire Mississippi Valley for France. The country is named Louisiana

1699 French priests settle in Cahokia (Illinois)

1701 Antoine Cadillac of France founds la ville d'Etroit (now Detroit)

1731 The French form the first permanent settlement in Indiana at Vincennes

1762 France cedes Upper Louisiana (Missouri) to Spain

1763 England acquires Wisconsin from France under the Treaty of Paris and takes possession of Michigan, Ohio, and Illinois after the French and Indian Wars

1764 Frenchmen Pierre Laclède Liguest and Auguste Chouteau found St. Louis, Missouri

1767 Daniel Boone makes his first journey of exploration in Kentucky

1772 The Watauga Association in Tennessee draws up one of the first written constitutions in America

1774 Harrodsburg is founded, the first permanent settlement in Kentucky

1775-83 Frontier leaders in Kentucky defend the state against Native American attacks throughout the Revolution

1776 The United States declares its independence from Britain

1778 The settlements of Cahokia and Kaskaskia are captured by U.S. forces

1783 Wisconsin becomes part of the United States

1788 Illinois becomes part of the United States

1792 Kentucky becomes the 15th state

1795 Native American wars in Ohio end with the Treaty of Greenville

1796 Tennessee becomes the 16th state

1800 Spain cedes Iowa to France. Congress establishes the Indiana Territory by dividing the Northwest Territory in two. Spain returns Louisiana to France, opening the way for the Louisiana Purchase

1803 Ohio becomes the 17th state. The United States acquires Iowa and Arkansas under the terms of the Louisiana Purchase

1811 General Harrison's forces defeat the Shawnee at the battle of Tippecanoe, Indiana

1812 Native Americans massacre many settlers at Fort Dearborn, Illinois

1813 Commodore Oliver Hazard Perry defeats the British fleet at the battle of Lake Erie

1815 Native American attacks cease following peacemaking at Portage des Sioux, Missouri

1816 Indiana becomes the 19th state

1818 Illinois becomes the 21st state. Chickasaw sell their lands east of the Missouri to the U.S. government

1821 Missouri becomes the 24th state

1832 The Ohio-Erie Canal is completed. Sauk and Fox tribes defeated in the Black Hawk War, Illinois

1833 Permanent settlement begins in Iowa

1836 Arkansas becomes the 25th state. The Cherokee are forced out of Tennessee

1837 Michigan becomes the 26th state

1845 Iron mining begins at Negaunee, Michigan. The Miami-Erie Canal is completed

1846 Iowa becomes the 29th state

1848 Wisconsin becomes the 30th state

1854 The Republican party is formally named at Jackson, Michigan, after its formation at Ripon, Wisconsin.

1861 Tennessee secedes from the Union at the outbreak of the Civil War. Missouri becomes a major battleground with the battles of Boonville and Wilson's Creek. Kentucky stays with the Union

European settlers were ▶ *frightened by Native Americans. Native Americans were disturbed to find wagon trains traveling across what had been open prairie, threatening an end to their freedom to roam and hunt as they pleased. This painting is by C. M. Russell.*

Into the unknown. In this ▶ *painting, artist George Caleb Bingham shows Daniel Boone leading a band of pioneers west. In the 1760s, Boone opened up what is now Kentucky.*

▼ Commodore Oliver Hazard Perry at a critical moment during the battle of Lake Erie on September 10, 1813. The British, under Captain Barclay, were defeated in the battle.

▲ A lithograph of the time portrays the Great Fire of Chicago, which destroyed much of the city on October 8, 1871. The damage was estimated at $200 million.

Driving them crazy! The ▶ Midwest not only built motor cars, it raced them, too. America's—and perhaps the world's—most famous race is the Indianapolis 500, which was first run in 1911. Average speeds then were about 75 mph. This 1910 poster advertises the thrills and spills of motor racing in Indianapolis.

1862 Kentucky becomes the war zone with a Union victory at Mill Springs, a Confederate win at Richmond, and a "draw" at Perryville

1866 Tennessee is the first state to be readmitted to the Union

1867 The first railroad runs from the Mississippi to Council Bluffs, Iowa

1870 Benjamin F. Goodrich begins rubber manufacture at Akron, Ohio

1871 Fire destroys much of Chicago; 300 people are killed

1887 First gas wells at Portland, Indiana; bauxite discovered at Little Rock, Arkansas

1890s Fights against private railroads and toll roads in Kentucky

1899 Robert E. Olds founds the first automobile factory in Detroit

1900 The Chicago Sanitary and Ship Canal is opened

1906 United States Steel Company builds a plant at Gary, Indiana. The town is named after U.S. Steel chairman Elbert Gary

1911 The first Indianapolis 500 motor race is run. Ray Harroun is the victor

1920s–30s The Great Depression leads to the collapse of many small farms

1921 First oil well in Arkansas at El Dorado begins production

1936 The gold depository at Fort Knox, Kentucky, is established

1942 Scientists led by Enrico Fermi set off the first controlled nuclear chain reaction at the University of Chicago

1957 National Guardsmen enforce integration at Little Rock Central High School

1968 Civil rights leader Rev. Martin Luther King, Jr., assassinated in Memphis, Tennessee

1970 Four students are killed by Ohio National Guardsmen during anti-Vietnam War demonstrations at Kent State University

1983 The first black mayor of Chicago, Harold Washington, is elected

Natural Wonders

If you thought that the middle of America was all flat farmland, you were wrong. There is farmland, of course—and plenty of it. But it varies from the rolling prairie of Illinois to the bluegrass of Kentucky, beloved by horse breeders.

Then there is the Midwest's magnificent shoreline. Lake Michigan's coastline boasts the colored cliffs at Picture Rock as well as the 17-mile-long Lakeshore Park. And there are the rivers. There are winding river gorges at the Dells, in Wisconsin, but the most striking river feature is the meeting of the mighty Mississippi and Ohio rivers at the southern tip of Illinois.

Other scenic wonders of the area include the Blue Hole, a remarkable artesian spring at Castalia, Ohio, producing 7 million gallons of water a day. Then there's Hocking Hills, Ohio, a state park that is also known as Little Yellowstone. It is filled with waterfalls and gorges, cliffs and chasms.

Lookout Mountain, Tennessee, is the Civil War's most picturesque battlefield, a 2,225-foot-high peak on which the Battle Above the Clouds was fought. At the other extreme is Mammoth Cave, Kentucky, a deep series of sandstone and limestone caverns containing arched domes, curtainlike formations, and a crystal-clear subterranean lake.

▲ Ohio's Hocking Hills State Park, known as Little Yellowstone, has among its attractions scenic waterfalls, cool gorges, strangely named caves and rock ledges, and steep cliffs.

▼ The Great Lakes are one of the most spectacular features of North America. Though now a trade route, Lake Huron still retains its natural beauty.

◄ The ridge of sand dunes near Michigan City is very fertile; even orchids grow there. The biggest dune of all is the 190-foot-high Mount Tom.

▼ Cliffs ring the coastlines of Lake Superior and Lake Michigan—among them, colored cliffs at Picture Rock and the 17-mile-long Lakeshore Park.

Flora and Fauna

This common skunk, with ▶ its white **V** marking, can grow to be ten pounds and 19 inches in length. The shy, nocturnal skunk secretes a foul-smelling spray when it is frightened or in danger. The spotted skunk—the smallest member of the skunk family—can climb trees. The hog-nosed skunk has a bare snout.

▼ Not King Cotton, but fluffy-headed cotton grass. It carpets meadows throughout the region and makes a pretty sight. Other vegetation includes bald cypress trees and majestic 100-foot Ozark chestnuts, now rare due to a blight that attacked them in the 1890s.

The wide-open spaces of the heart of America are attractive to creatures that prefer a lot of room in which to live. These include bears, deer, game birds like the pheasant, quail, and ruffed grouse, and huge flocks of Canada geese. The early settlers may well have thought they were in Nature's larder, for the region is also home to wild rice, berries grow in the boggy areas, and the river fish include delicious muskies, giant members of the pike family. Cotton grass is everywhere, and other regional specialties include the wood thrush, the snowshoe hare, and the bald cypress.

Skunks—perhaps North America's most unpopular mammal—are common here. Far more appealing is the oriole, a brightly colored bird with a loud musical song. The common loon, a black-and-white spotted diving bird, may also be seen as it hunts for fish in remote lakes.

Two species of tree have particular associations with this region. A medium-size tree reaching 100 feet in height, the American chestnut was especially useful to pioneers. It gave a plentiful harvest of nuts, tannin could be produced from its bark, and its wood was very durable. Sadly, this species has been nearly wiped out by chestnut blight. The tamarack, or eastern larch, is also known as the hackmatack and grows up to 60 feet tall. It is deciduous and has particularly tough roots. Native Americans of the region, who were known for their beautiful and functional canoes, made rope out of tamarack roots to bind them.

▲ Known as tamarack, hackmatack, or eastern larch, this pretty tree grows into a 60-foot pyramid. Native Americans used its tough roots to make rope for their canoes.

◀ The call of the common loon has often alarmed people sleeping outdoors at night. More often heard than seen, the loon lives in remote lakeland areas. It eats fish.

▲ The melodious Baltimore oriole. These birds bind grass to make hanging nests that can be perilous in high winds.

The Adventurers

Many men and women from these states made their mark on American history. They seem to typify the adventurous spirit of the region.

David Crockett (1786–1836) A tavern keeper's son from Rogersville, Kentucky, David Crockett (popularly known as Davy) spent just four days at school, then ran away for three years. He joined the army and fought the Creek tribe. After living as a hunter in the wilderness, he served in the Tennessee legislature from 1821 to 1824 and was elected to the House of Representatives in 1827. In 1835, after losing his seat in Congress, he led a party of settlers to Texas, where he soon joined the revolutionaries at the Alamo. He died there in the massacre on March 6, 1836.

Abraham Lincoln (1809–65) Born near Hodgenville, Kentucky, Lincoln grew up in a log cabin and had only a year's formal schooling. While working in a store in New Salem, Illinois, he studied law in his spare time. He eventually went into practice in Springfield in 1837. An imposing six feet four inches tall, a good speaker, and an outspoken opponent of slavery, he was elected to Congress in 1847 and became president in 1860. He piloted the Union cause to victory in the Civil War but was assassinated in 1865.

Mark Twain (1835–1910) America's greatest humorist, Mark Twain's real name was Samuel Langhorne Clemens. He was born in Florida, Missouri, the son of a poor couple. He worked as a printer but then decided to become a river pilot instead. This experience stimulated him to write novels like *Tom Sawyer* and *Huckleberry Finn*. The name Mark Twain, which he first used as a newspaperman, came from his riverboat days. Mark twain means two fathoms, a measure of depth in water.

Thomas Edison (1847–1931) Born in Milan, Ohio, the young Edison had only three months' formal education. He became a telegrapher and invented an unsuccessful vote-recording machine before finally getting a big cash grant for improving the ticker-tape machine. In his own workshops, he was able to improve the telephone, invent the phonograph and movie camera, and introduce electric light bulbs. He also designed the world's first power station.

◄ *King of the wild frontier. This is how painter J. G. Chapman saw frontiersman Davy Crockett, whose exploits ended at the Alamo.*

▲ *Public adulation for the imposing figure of Abraham Lincoln, the president from Kentucky who abolished slavery in the 1860s*

Mark Twain—the Missouri ▶
printer who was to become
America's best-known
humorist. His masterpieces
are Tom Sawyer *and*
Huckleberry Finn.

▼ *Inventor Thomas Edison,*
from Ohio, listening to a
phonograph. A lack of
schooling did not stop him
from achieving greatness.

John "Duke" Wayne ▶
(1907–79) made over 80 films
during his movie career. The
number one western star, he
won an Oscar for his role in
True Grit *(1969).*

▼ *Rock 'n' roll star Elvis*
Presley (1935–77) was born
in Mississippi but lived in
a mansion called Graceland
in Memphis, Tennessee.

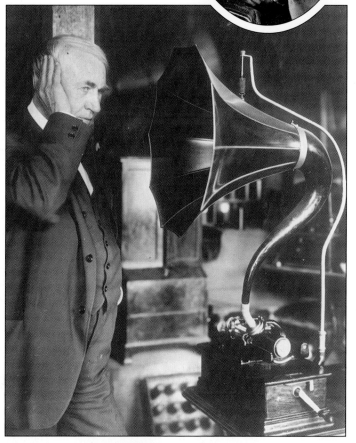

▼ *Boxing champion*
Muhammad Ali (1942–   )
was born Cassius Clay in
Louisville, Kentucky. In
1964, he won the World
Heavyweight title.
A natural showman,
his slogan was "I
am the greatest."

Frank Lloyd Wright (1867–1959) Born in Richland Center, Wisconsin, Wright was an imaginative architect who influenced the design of many American cities and homes.

Wilbur and Orville Wright (1867–1912, 1871–1948) Born in Indiana and Ohio, respectively, the Wright brothers made the first flight in a power-driven, heavier-than-air machine of their own design. They first flew their "airplane" on December 17, 1903.

Edna Ferber (1887–1968) Well-known American novelist from Kalamazoo, Michigan, whose books portray many types of Americans. Among her most famous are the Pulitzer Prize-winning *So Big*, *Showboat*, and *Giant*.

Ralph Johnson Bunche (1904–71) Born in Detroit, Michigan, Bunche worked for the U.S. government and the United Nations. He was the first black man to head a division in the Department of State and was awarded the Nobel Peace Prize in 1950 for his work with the UN.

John Glenn (1921–   ) Born in Cambridge, Ohio, Glenn was the first American to orbit the earth, on February 20, 1962. Glenn was elected senator in 1974.

The Great Cities

Detroit, Michigan, or Motown, as it is called, is the home of America's automobile industry. The factories on which its fame and fortune were based still welcome visitors. Another attraction is the Henry Ford Museum and Greenfield Village in Dearborn. Greenfield is a reproduction of an early American village created by Ford. The striking Civic Center is popular, as are trips across the Detroit River to Windsor, in Canada.

Chicago The world's tallest office and residential buildings dominate the Chicago, Illinois, skyline. Down at street level, the old Loop Railway still rattles around, as restless as the city itself. Chicago survived a great fire in 1871 to become a communications center on the shores of Lake Michigan. Now it is also a cultural center—with some excellent museums like the Field Museum and a superb planetarium and aquarium.

▲ *Skyscrapers really live up to their name in Chicago, which rivals New York for the tallest buildings and most imposing skyline.*

The Gateway Arch, ▶ *designed by a Finn, soars above the Old Courthouse—a symbol of St. Louis and its pioneering spirit.*

▲ Paddle steamers ply the Mississippi around Memphis, Tennessee. This city is regarded as the birthplace of the blues.

◄ Detroit is known as Motown because of its link with the automobile industry. A recent addition to the city has been this elevated mass-transit system.

Another riverside city ▶ with a musical tradition is Nashville, best known for country and western music.

Memphis A one-time Native American settlement that President Andrew Jackson helped to found, Memphis, Tennessee, is a commercial center with excellent art galleries. Its huge new pyramid and the equally new Civil Rights Center prove that Memphis is more than just a way station for Elvis Presley fans flocking to his home at Graceland or a haven for lovers of the blues.

Nashville An up-to-date manufacturing and financial center with a rich history, Nashville, Tennessee, is best known as the heart of the country and western music scene. Its headquarters are at the famous Grand Ole Opry. President Andrew Jackson's lovely former home, the Hermitage, is just out of town.

St. Louis It was only a fur-trading post 200 years ago, when it was named after the French King Louis XV. But St. Louis, Missouri, is now a business and cultural center on the banks of the Mississippi. Its most famous sight is the 630-foot-high Gateway Arch. An observation deck atop the arch provides panoramic views of the city, encompassing the Old Courthouse and Old Cathedral.

4 The West

The extraordinary topography of the West—where the plains give way to the giant Rocky Mountains, and the Rockies give way to the desert—should have broken the hearts of the earliest westbound travelers. Instead, the area has produced a succession of equally extraordinary characters.

Contrary to popular belief, the climate is sometimes a hindrance to farmers rather than a help, with its often icy winters and dryness. Men and women worked hard to turn this area into the nation's breadbasket, irrigating the deserts by means of a series of dams along the Colorado River. Meanwhile, other residents worked equally hard to tame the Rockies and recover the minerals and precious metals from the soil.

To the Europeans and easterners who immigrated here, this was a new country—and in some ways, it still is. There is a museum in New Mexico that claims, proudly, to have exhibits "dating right back to the 1930s." But the stone arrowheads that litter the deserts of the same state and the Native American carved drawings that adorn the rocks speak of those who lived here before.

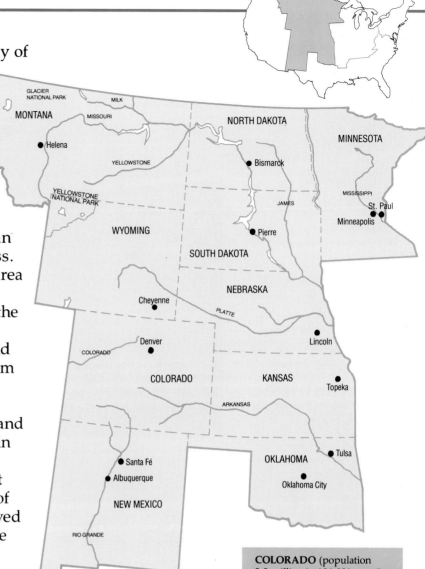

▼ *In this painting by Frederic Remington, Native American riders drag away their wounded after raiding a wagon train. Settlers threatened Native American life-styles.*

COLORADO (population 3.3 million in 104,091 sq mi)
Climate: sunny, dry summers; cold winters
State flower: Rocky Mountain columbine
State bird: lark bunting
Capital: Denver
Industries: mining, agriculture, manufacturing, aerospace, electronics, tourism
Entered Union: August 1, 1876

NORTH DAKOTA (population 0.64 million in 70,702 sq mi)
Climate: continental, with wide range of temperature; moderate rainfall
State flower: wild prairie rose
State bird: western meadowlark
Capital: Bismarck
Industries: agriculture (especially wheat and flax), livestock, mining, farm machinery
Entered Union: November 2, 1889

▲ *Soaring spires in the Mile-High City. This skyline is in Denver, Colorado, which lies in the shadow of the mighty Rocky Mountains.*

SOUTH DAKOTA (population 0.7 million in 77,116 sq mi)
Climate: hot summers, cold winters in the west, milder and more humid in the east
State flower: pasqueflower
State bird: ring-necked pheasant
Capital: Pierre
Industries: agriculture (especially cattle, grain), manufacturing, food processing
Entered Union: November 2, 1889

KANSAS (population 2.5 million in 82,277 sq mi)
Climate: cold winters, warm summers, changeable
State flower: native sunflower
State bird: western meadowlark
Capital: Topeka
Industries: agriculture (especially cattle, grain), manufacturing, printing and publishing
Entered Union: January 19, 1861

MINNESOTA (population 4.4 million in 84,402 sq mi)
Climate: temperate, but with frosty winters
State flower: pink and white lady's slipper
State bird: common loon
Capital: St. Paul
Industries: agriculture (especially corn, wheat), fishing, mining, chemicals, manufacturing
Entered Union: May 11, 1858

MONTANA (population 0.8 million in 147,046 sq mi)
Climate: harsh winters east of the divide, milder in the west
State flower: bitterroot
State bird: western meadowlark
Capital: Helena
Industries: silver and copper mining and smelting, oil and gas, agriculture, lumber
Entered Union: November 8, 1889

NEBRASKA (population 1.6 million in 77,355 sq mi)
Climate: dry, with harsh winters, hot summers

State flower: goldenrod
State bird: western meadowlark
Capital: Lincoln
Industries: agriculture (especially grain, cattle), food processing, aerospace, manufacturing, metal products
Entered Union: March 1, 1867

NEW MEXICO (population 1.5 million in 121,593 sq mi)
Climate: sunny, hot summers; cold in the mountains, dry
State flower: yucca
State bird: roadrunner
Capital: Sante Fe
Industries: minerals, agriculture (especially cattle), tourism, lumber, research, printing, machinery
Entered Union: January 6, 1912

OKLAHOMA (population 3.1 million in 69,919 sq mi)
Climate: dry, with warm summers, mild winters
State flower: mistletoe
State bird: scissor-tailed flycatcher
Capital: Oklahoma City
Industries: manufacturing, mineral and energy exploration and production, agriculture, printing and publishing
Entered Union: November 16, 1907

WYOMING (population 0.45 million in 97,809 sq mi)
Climate: semi- or true desert conditions
State flower: Indian paintbrush
State bird: meadowlark
Capital: Cheyenne
Industries: agriculture (especially hay, cattle), mining, wood products, tourism, clay and glass products
Entered Union: July 10, 1890

◄ *The spectacular scenery of Wyoming, where horses graze against a backdrop of the Teton mountains amid endless grassy prairies*

◄ *The living desert. An evergreen yucca, the state flower of New Mexico, flourishes in sparse soil. It develops a spike of pale flowers.*

Historical Highlights

The history of the region is a real-life adventure story. Its heroes were the intrepid explorers. Its villains, perhaps, were the rulers of Europe, arguing over the ownership of tracts of land bigger than their own nations. And its victims, sadly, were those Native Americans whose way of life was destroyed as the country developed.

Just as greed inspired European leaders, so it also motivated some of the pioneers who found their way out West. But there were other motives, too: from the challenge of the unknown to the need for space or to escape from persecution. The major dates of the region's history chart the pioneers' progress.

▲ "To the Black Hills or bust" was the motto of miners such as this, rushing to exploit the goldfields of South Dakota in 1874.

▼ The railroads played a vital part in opening up the West in the 1860s. This lithograph of an "express train" is by Currier & Ives.

1540-42 Francisco Vasquez de Coronado of Spain searches for gold in New Mexico, Kansas, and Oklahoma

1610 Pedro de Peralta of Spain founds Santa Fe, New Mexico

1659–61 Pierre Radisson and Médard Chouart des Groseilliers of France explore Minnesota (the Northern Plains)

1679 Greysolon's expedition charts the west end of Lake Superior

1680 Pueblo Native Americans drive out the Spanish from New Mexico. The French explorer Father Hennepin sights the falls of St. Anthony in Minnesota

1692 de Vargas claims New Mexico for Spain

1706 Juan de Uribarri claims Colorado for Spain. Francisco Cuervo y Valdes of Spain founds Albuquerque, New Mexico

1714 Frenchman Sieur de Bourgmont travels up the Missouri to the mouth of the Platte River

1720 The Pawnee defeat the Spanish along the Platte River, Nebraska

1762 France cedes Nebraska to Spain

1783 Britain grants lands east of the Mississippi to the United States

1800 Spain cedes Nebraska to France

1803 At least parts of all the present states of the West become U.S. territory under the terms of the Louisiana Purchase

1804–6 Explorers and mapmakers Meriwether Lewis and William Clark explore the new Louisiana Territories as far as the Pacific Ocean

1807 John Colter explores the Yellowstone area of Wyoming

1812 Scots and Irish settlers found the first permanent settlement in North Dakota. Robert Stuart discovers the South Pass over the Rockies

1817 Frenchman La Framboise establishes the first permanent settlement in South Dakota at Fort Pierre

1818 The United States acquires what is now southeastern North Dakota from Britain

1819–22 The U.S. Army establishes Fort St. Anthony, now Fort Snelling, in Minnesota

1822 William Becknell establishes the Santa Fe Trail from Independence, Missouri, to Santa Fe, New Mexico

1824 Fort Gibson and Fort Towson, the first military posts in Oklahoma, are established

1827 Colonel Leavenworth establishes Fort Leavenworth, Kansas

1830–42 Mass migration of Native Americans; the Five Civilized Tribes move into Oklahoma

The Native American woman guide Sacajawea points out the lay of the land to the explorers and mapmakers Lewis and Clark. They explored to the Pacific in 1804–6.

▲ Major General George Armstrong Custer adopts a heroic pose. He was defeated and killed at the battle of Little Big Horn in 1876.

1833 Captain Benjamin de Bonneville maps Wyoming and discovers oil east of the Wind River
1843 The Great Migration along the Oregon Trail begins
1846 General Stephen Kearny controls New Mexico in the Mexican War
1848 The United States takes western Colorado after the Mexican War. Spain cedes New Mexico to the United States
1850s Armed conflicts over the slavery question give rise to the name Bleeding Kansas
1851 Native Americans give up rights to lands in Iowa and Minnesota
1858 Minnesota becomes the 32nd state. A gold rush starts near Denver at Cherry Creek, Colorado

▼ This painting by Frederic Remington shows Custer shortly before his defeat at Little Big Horn. It is called Custer's Last Charge.

Stone giants. The faces of ▶ four famous American presidents—Washington, Lincoln, Jefferson, and Theodore Roosevelt—have been carved into the side of Mount Rushmore, South Dakota.

1861 Kansas becomes the 34th state
1862 Troops and militiamen put down a Sioux uprising in Minnesota
1863 North Dakota is opened for homesteading. The "farming bonanza" lasts until 1875
1864 Congress establishes the Montana Territory. Colonel Kit Carson defeats the Mescalero Apache and the Navajo in New Mexico
1865 The Union Pacific Railway builds west of Omaha
1867 The Union Pacific Railway enters Wyoming. Nebraska becomes the 37th state
1868 The Laramie Treaty ends Chief Red Cloud's war in Wyoming Territory
1872 The first National Park is established at Yellowstone in Idaho, Montana, and Wyoming
1875 Conflict breaks out between Sioux in the Black Hills and gold prospectors who are exploiting Native American lands

1876 The Sioux and Cheyenne defeat and kill Colonel Custer and more than 200 soldiers at Little Big Horn, Montana. Colorado becomes the 38th state. Wild Bill Hickok killed in a saloon in Deadwood
1880-83 Railroads cross Montana north-south and east-west
1883 The first oil well in production at Lander, Wyoming
1889 North Dakota becomes the 39th state; South Dakota, the 40th; Montana, the 41st. The Mayo Clinic founded in Minnesota
1890 Wyoming becomes the 44th state. A great drought in Nebraska leads to the collapse of land prices. Chief Big Foot and 152 Sioux killed at Wounded Knee. Congress creates Oklahoma Territory, formerly Indian Territory
1892 Cattle rustling wars in Johnson County, Wyoming
1894 Gas and oil fields start production in Kansas
1903 Helium discovered at Dexter, Kansas
1906 The U.S. Mint begins operation in Denver, Colorado
1907 Oklahoma becomes the 46th state
1910 Glacier National Park in Montana established
1912 New Mexico becomes the 47th state
1915 The Rocky Mountain National Park established
1927 Work on Mount Rushmore in South Dakota begins under sculptor Gutzon Borglum
1930s The depression hits small farmers; droughts and dust storms devastate South Dakota and Kansas
1945 The first atom bomb is exploded at Alamogordo, New Mexico
1956 Water storage projects begin on the Colorado River
1977 The Solar Energy Research Institute founded at Denver, Colorado

Natural Wonders

As the plains give way to the mountains and then to the deserts of the West, the scenery becomes more dramatic and the natural wonders more wonderful. Among these are the group of weird sandstone formations in Colorado, called the "garden of the gods" by Native Americans. Then there are the man-made wonders. These include the carvings on Mount Rushmore in South Dakota and the rock pillars of the Pipestone National Monument in Minnesota, where Native Americans mined clay for their peace pipes.

Old Faithful is the most dramatic sight in Yellowstone National Park, which spans three states—Idaho, Montana, and Wyoming. This massive geyser spouts thousands of gallons of steaming water 100 feet into the air every 50 to 80 minutes. Old Faithful is one of many such geysers in the area, but it is surely the best known. To the south, the Tetons are one of the most spectacular mountain ranges in North America, with principal peak Grand Teton rising 13,770 feet above sea level. The Sand Dunes of Colorado, covering an area of 30 square miles, are the mightiest dunes in the United States, soaring up to 800 feet above a valley near Alamosa. They change shape constantly because of wind erosion. They also attract spectacular lightning storms that turn their natural color to glorious pinks and mauves.

The Carlsbad Caverns in New Mexico are the largest underground chambers in the world. The limestone caves, with their strange rock formations, are a popular tourist attraction. Look out for the vast colonies of bats!

American greats carved in granite on Mount Rushmore. The likenesses of the presidents are the work of sculptor Gutzon Borglum.

◀ *Looking more like a snowfield than a desert, the White Sands of New Mexico are a vast, rolling sea of dunes formed of glittering gypsum crystals.*

▼ *Cowboy country. The buttes and badlands of the Dakotas and Montana, eroded and forbidding, are a familiar movie setting.*

▲ *Spectacular scenery in the Teton Mountains, along the Continental Divide*

▼ *Being lowered in a bucket was once the only way into the spectacular Carlsbad Caverns. Today, an elevator follows the stalactites down.*

▲ *Old Faithful spouts jets of sulfurous steam every 50 to 80 minutes without fail. One of many geysers in the area, it is the most popular attraction in Yellowstone National Park.*

Flora and Fauna

As the wheat fields give way to mountains and deserts, so the flora and fauna of the West undergo a dramatic change. As you head into New Mexico, for example, you may find coyotes lurking among the cacti. And watch where you walk, because there are snakes aplenty. Look out, too, for deer, bears, porcupines, sandhill cranes, and Mexican ducks.

This is a beautiful region, made even more attractive by the variety of its plants and shrubs. Among those that grow here are the purple-leafed gum tree, the wild prairie rose, the blackjack shrubs, and the imaginatively named Indian paintbrush flower. One of the most distinctive plants is the yucca. An evergreen member of the agave family, the yucca has a wooded trunk and stiff, narrow, pointed leaves with sawlike edges. Its pale, bell-like flowers sit on spiky stems. They open at night and are strongly scented. The American, or flowering, dogwood with its hard, heavy wood is an attractive winter tree, growing up to 40 feet high.

◄ Drifts of blossoms color the western landscape as the dogwoods bloom early in the year. Their flowers produce a bright red fruit.

The American bison is often (incorrectly) called a buffalo. It was almost wiped out by 19th-century hunters but is now protected. Its huge, bearded head and humped shoulders give it a fierce appearance, and it has a temper to match. A gentler creature is the pronghorn antelope. Unlike other horned animals, it sheds only the bony covering of its horns every year. These horns, coupled with keen eyesight, protect it from wolves and coyotes. The pronghorn can also travel pretty quickly when it needs to. Its ability to reach 60 miles per hour in a short sprint makes it the fastest-moving mammal in North America.

◄ *The American antelope is not strictly an antelope at all. This pronghorn actually has no close relatives among the deer family. Despite its small size, it can outpace most other animals. As it browses, it keeps an eye out for predators.*

▲ *A bristling war machine, the porcupine rustles its way through the pine forests, ready to raise its barbed, arrowlike quills in self-defense. It can grow up to three feet in length.*

◄ *Elegant inhabitants of this region's waters are the steely colored sandhill cranes. Their tall silhouettes can be seen among the reeds and on wooded riverbanks as they hunt fish.*

▼ *The shaggy bison was prized by Native American and European hunters alike, both for its hide and for the buffalo meat that it provided. Hunted until it was almost extinct, this massive beast is now protected.*

The Achievers

Some of the sons and daughters of the region can, at first glance, seem larger than life. Like the other pioneers who carved out this land, they were achievers, endowed with the determination to get things done.

Sitting Bull (c. 1831–90) One of America's most famous Native American chiefs, this South Dakotan was originally known as Slow. He was renamed Sitting Bull for his bravery in a tribal war. As medicine man and leader of the Hunkpapa Sioux tribe, he taught his people to fight effectively. This helped lead to the annihilation of Custer and his men by Sioux warriors under Crazy Horse at the battle of Little Big Horn on June 25, 1876. Sitting Bull and his son died resisting arrest in 1890.

Jack Dempsey (1895–1983) The most popular heavyweight boxing champion of all time was born in Manassa, Colorado, and began fighting in 1914 as the "Manassa Mauler." He held the World Heavyweight title from 1919 to 1926, eventually losing it to Gene Tunney. In a rematch in 1927, Tunney survived a controversial 14-second count to keep the title.

Amelia Earhart (1897–1937) Born in Atchison, Kansas, Earhart was the most famous woman aviator of all time. She was the first woman to cross the Atlantic by airplane (1928) and the first woman to make a solo flight across the Atlantic (1932). She was the first *person* to fly alone from Honolulu to California (1935). In 1937, during an attempt to fly around the world, her plane was lost. Her fate remains a mystery.

Charles Lindbergh (1902–74) America's most famous airman was born in Detroit and grew up in Little Falls, Minnesota, where he studied engineering. But Lindbergh decided to become a barnstormer and fairground stunt flyer. Later, he joined the army and ran an airmail service. In 1927, he flew his plane, the *Spirit of St. Louis*, nonstop from New York to Paris to win a $25,000 prize. Other record-breaking flights followed.

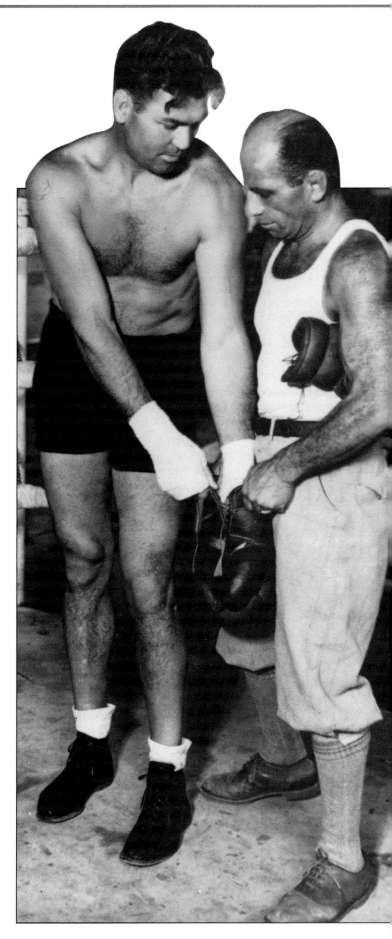

▲ Billy the Kid (1859–81), born Henry McCarty but often known as William H. Bonney, was a much-feared 19th-century outlaw.

◄ Putting on the gloves is Jack Dempsey, the Colorado boxer regarded as the most popular heavyweight champion of all time.

William Mayo (1819–1911) Head of the family whose work led to a decrease in postoperative death rates. The family also founded the famous Mayo Clinic in Rochester, Minnesota.

Lewis Wallace (1827–1905) A soldier, statesman, lawyer, and author from Brookville, Indiana, Lew Wallace wrote the novel *Ben Hur*.

Wild Bill Hickok (1837–76) James Butler Hickok, from Troy Grove, Illinois, was a skillful marksman, scout, and guerrilla fighter. Hickok made his mark in clashes with both Native Americans and outlaw gangs who roamed the Wild West.

Crazy Horse (c. 1842–77) A chief of the Oglala Sioux, he led the refusal by the tribe to enter a reservation in 1875. This began a long war against the U.S. cavalry. He commanded the Sioux at the battle of Little Big Horn in 1876.

Carry Nation (1846–1911) Born in Kentucky, she gained fame for temperance (anti-liquor) activities while living in Kansas. She was known for smashing saloons with a hatchet.

Georgia O'Keeffe (1887–1986) Noted American artist O'Keeffe was born in Wisconsin but lived in New Mexico for many years. The Southwest influenced her colorful paintings.

▲ The guy who created Guys and Dolls, *novelist Damon Runyon (1884–1946). Born in Manhattan, Kansas, he wrote about Manhattan, New York.*

St. Paul, Minnesota, ▶ *native, author F. Scott Fitzgerald (1896–1940), a novelist who wrote of the Roaring Twenties life-style, is seen here with his wife, Zelda.*

The Great Cities

The Twin Cities, facing each other across the upper reaches of the Mississippi, are hardly identical twins. **Saint Paul**, Minnesota, is a conservative state capital, while **Minneapolis** is one of the world's most beautiful cities, noteworthy for its 11 lakes and clean water. There are also 156 parks in Minneapolis, which make for unpolluted air. The Twin Cities is a major cultural center, boasting concert halls, great theater, and a trio of major art galleries.

Albuquerque Officially New Mexico's only large city, Albuquerque has spread in many directions from the banks of the Rio Grande in the last 50 years. It has become a major scientific and educational center. The Old Town Plaza, with its fortresslike San Felipe de Neri church, is the symbol of old Albuquerque. The Museum of Anthropology at the city's University of New Mexico traces the earliest history of this region.

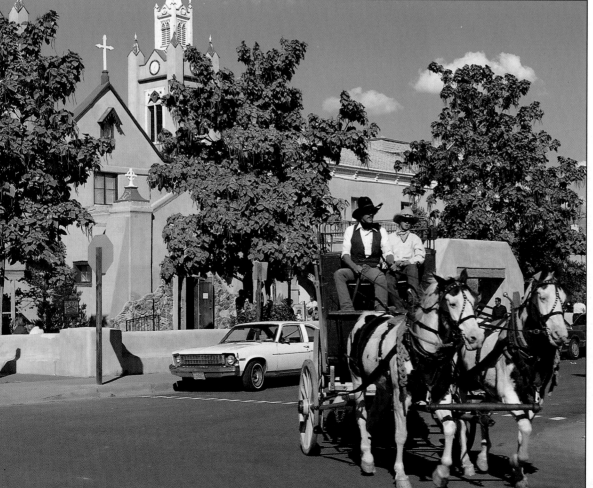

◀ *With its cowboy culture, Indian shops, and Spanish-style buildings in Old Town Plaza, the city of Albuquerque, New Mexico, is a true melting pot.*

▼ *One of the world's most beautiful cities, Minneapolis is renowned for its wide streets and for its numerous parks and lakes. It is an important trade and financial center, but its cultural life also thrives. America's biggest summer festival, the Minneapolis Aquatennial, takes place in July, while St. Paul stages a "twin" Winter Carnival.*

▲ *Oklahoma City is famous for modern architecture, but it also has a rich pioneering history. As it is built on top of an oil field, its future seems secure. It is home to the National Cowboy Hall of Fame.*

▲ *Seen against the spectacular backdrop of the Rockies, Denver, Colorado, is now a leading business center.*

▼ *St. Paul faces Minneapolis across the Mississippi. The Twin Cities is a thriving cultural center.*

Denver The Mile-High City in Colorado is accurately named. The 13th step of the western entrance to the gold-crowned capitol building is exactly one mile above sea level. It also offers a beautiful view of the Rockies. The capitol, built in the late 19th century, is a smaller replica of the U.S. Capitol in Washington. In the latter half of this century, Denver has really boomed as a business center. Fittingly, the town's star attraction is the U.S. Mint.

Oklahoma City *Oklahoma* means "home of the red men" in the Choctaw language. But it was black gold—oil—that put Oklahoma City on the map. There is even an oil well beneath the capitol building! A walking tour of the city takes in the striking modern architecture and fine shopping malls, but beneath the modern veneer, this is still a pioneer town.

5 The Far West, Alaska, and Hawaii

It is a plot of which any Hollywood film producer would be proud. Intrepid explorers crossing vast tracts of land from the East meet up with brave mariners who have sailed around the world to reach the West Coast. Together, they create a new nation. They overcome climatic extremes, floods, and even earthquakes, to found great cities. People come to the new nation from places as far apart as the frozen lands of the north and the islands of the southern Pacific Ocean.

It is the story of an extraordinary part of America: the booming West Coast and the Pacific states, Alaska and Hawaii. And, indeed, this area *is* booming. If California declared its independence tomorrow, it would be the sixth wealthiest nation on earth.

People who live on the West Coast have great individuality. The desire to do things their own way brought many of them there. This is why the Mormons moved to Utah . . . just as this was the reason for the original journey of the Pilgrims to the New World. But not only can you be yourself in the Far West; there is a terrain and a climate to suit every taste. The woodsman in Washington State, the Arizona cowboy, the Alaskan oilman, the Hawaiian pineapple farmer— they all have completed the journey that the Vikings and the Pilgrim Fathers began. They have found America.

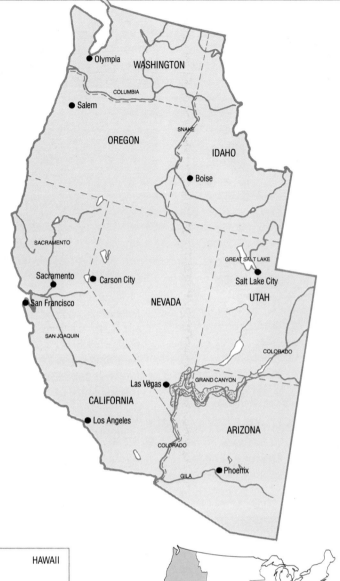

▲ *Journeys to the West were not always easy. This 1871 engraving shows a welcome break in a wagon train's cross-country progress.*

ALASKA (population 0.56 million in 591,000 sq mi)
Climate: mild, wet, and snowy in the south, very cold and dry in the north
State flower: forget-me-not
State bird: willow ptarmigan
Capital: Juneau
Industries: fishing, game, furs, lumber, wood products, oil, gas, tourism
Entered Union: January 3, 1959

ARIZONA (population 3.7 million in 114,000 sq mi)
Climate: great extremes, very dry
State flower: blossom of the saguaro cactus
State bird: cactus wren
Capital: Phoenix
Industries: manufacturing, mining, agriculture (especially cotton, citrus fruits, cattle), aerospace
Entered Union: February 14, 1912

CALIFORNIA (population 29.8 million in 158,706 sq mi)
Climate: south coast mild, north coast mild and cooler, extremes in the interior
State flower: golden poppy
State bird: California valley quail
Capital: Sacramento
Industries: agriculture, manufacturing, tourism, fishing, electronics, entertainment, aerospace
Entered Union: September 9, 1850

HAWAII (population 1.1 million in 6,471 sq mi)
Climate: subtropical, with wide variation in rainfall
State flower: yellow hibiscus
State bird: Hawaiian goose
Capital: Honolulu
Industries: tourism, fishing, agriculture (especially sugar, pineapple), clothing
Entered Union: August 21, 1959

IDAHO (population 1 million in 83,564 sq mi)
Climate: mild throughout most of state; drier, colder in southeast
State flower: syringa
State bird: mountain bluebird
Capital: Boise
Industries: agriculture, manufacturing, tourism, lumber, mining, electronics, chemicals
Entered Union: July 3, 1890

NEVADA (population 1.2 million in 110,561 sq mi)
Climate: cold winters and cool summers in the mountains, hot with mild winters in the deserts, extremely dry
State flower: sagebrush
State bird: mountain bluebird
Capital: Carson City
Industries: gambling, tourism, mining, manufacturing, agriculture
Entered Union: October 31, 1864

OREGON (population 2.8 million in 97,073 sq mi)
Climate: mild and varied, more extreme in the interior
State flower: Oregon grape
State bird: western meadowlark
Capital: Salem
Industries: forestry, agriculture, manufacturing, food processing, printing
Entered Union: February 14, 1859

UTAH (population 1.7 million in 84,899 sq mi)
Climate: dry, ranging from warm desert in southwest to alpine in northeast
State flower: sego lily
State bird: sea gull
Capital: Salt Lake City
Industries: manufacturing, construction, mining, electronics, defense products
Entered Union: January 4, 1896

WASHINGTON (population 4.9 million in 68,139 sq mi)
Climate: mild, dominated by the Pacific Ocean, protected by the Rockies
State flower: western rhododendron
State bird: willow goldfinch
Capital: Olympia
Industries: aerospace, forest products, food products, fishing, agriculture, paper
Entered Union: November 11, 1889

▲ *A peaceful corner of one of the world's most famous stretches of sand. This is Waikiki Beach, in Honolulu, Hawaii. The beaches of Hawaii offer some of the greatest surfing in the world.*

▼ *The City by the Bay is San Francisco, whose setting is among the most beautiful in the world. This aerial view includes Oakland Bay Bridge.*

▲ *Mountain splendor. The moon rises above the granite peaks of Cathedral Rocks, famous landmarks in Yosemite National Park, California.*

Historical Highlights

Just as the Eastern Seaboard was first explored by the sailing ships of European fortune seekers, so the West Coast attracted its own nautical adventurers. In the 16th century—hundreds of year after Chinese sailors first did it—the Englishman Sir Francis Drake sailed up the California coast. But it was the Spaniards who first settled the West. Dane Vitus Bering explored Alaska while Captain James Cook of England reached the Hawaiian Islands. Here, along the Pacific rim, the creation of the nation reached its climax—uniting not just the European settlers and the Native Americans, but peoples as varied as the Alaskan Eskimo and Polynesian islanders. Important dates in this process are recorded here.

1539 The Spanish Franciscan priest de Niza visits Arizona

1542 Juan Rodriguez Cabrillo of Spain explores San Diego Bay

1572 Sir Francis Drake explores the California coast and claims it for England, calling it New Albion

1602 The explorer Sebastian Vizcaino urges Spain to colonize California

1692 Father Kino, a Jesuit, begins missionary work in the Santa Cruz and San Pedro valleys, Arizona

1741 The Dane Vitus Bering's expedition lands in Alaska

1769 Establishment of the first California mission, San Diego de Alcala, by Spanish Franciscan Father Junipero Serra

1775 Spaniards Heceta and Bodega y Quadra land on Washington soil. Native Americans attack and destroy Franciscan mission at San Diego

1776 Spanish settlers from New Spain (Mexico) reach the site of San Francisco. Friar Gaces is the first European in Nevada. Padre Francisco De Escalante and Dominguez of Spain explore Utah. Tucson, Arizona, is founded as a fort

1778 Captain Cook reaches Hawaiian Islands. He names them the Sandwich Islands

1809 David Thompson establishes the first fur-trading post in Idaho

1810 British and Canadians establish a fur-trading post near Spokane, Washington. King Kamehameha I unifies the Hawaiian Islands

1812 Russian fur traders build Fort Ross. Earthquake destroys Mission San Juan Capistrano in California

1818 The United States and Britain agree to joint occupation of Washington and Oregon

1819 A treaty between the United States and Spain fixes the southern border of Oregon. Death of King Kamehameha I of Hawaii

1820 Christian missionaries arrive to convert the Hawaiians

1822 California becomes part of New Spain (Mexico)

1824-25 A treaty between the United States, Britain, and Russia recognizes the southern boundary of Alaska at 54° 40′ north

1827 Catholic missionaries arrive in Hawaii, only to be thrown out in 1831. First sawmill in Pacific Northwest opens at Fort Vancouver.

Sixteenth-century explorer ▶ Sir Francis Drake with some of his spoils. Drake explored the coast of California.

1835 Ladd & Company establishes the first sugar plantation on Hawaii

1841 The first party of overland settlers, the Bidwell Bartleson party, arrives in California after crossing the Rocky Mountains on the Oregon Trail

1846 A treaty between the United States and Britain establishes the Canadian border along the 49th parallel. American rebels raise the "bear" flag of the California republic over Sonoma, declaring their independence from Mexico

1847 The first Mormons, led by Brigham Young, arrive in Utah to build a settlement by the Great Salt Lake

1848 Gold is found at Sutters Mill, California. Mexico yields California, Nevada, Utah, and Arizona to the United States

1849 Gold rush in California. Mormons found their state, Deseret, in Utah

1850 California becomes the 31st state

1855–58 Native American wars in Washington

1859 Oregon becomes the 33rd state

1861 Telegraph lines meet at Salt Lake City. Apache under Cochise begin terrorizing settlers in Arizona. First transcontinental telegram sent from Sacramento to Washington, D.C.

1864 Nevada becomes the 36th state

1867 The United States purchases Alaska from Russia for $7.2 million

1869 The first transcontinental railway completed at Promontory Point, Utah

1877 Chief Joseph and the Nez Percé surrender, ending Native American wars caused by relocation from their home in Oregon to a reservation in Idaho

1883 The Northern Pacific Railroad links with the East in Washington

1886 Geronimo and the Apache surrender at Skeleton Canyon in Arizona, marking the end of Native American fighting

1887 Land boom in California

1889 Washington becomes the 42nd state

1890 Idaho becomes the 43rd state. The Mormons prohibit polygamy

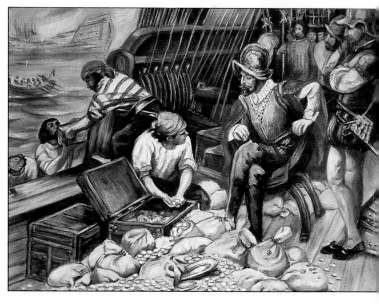

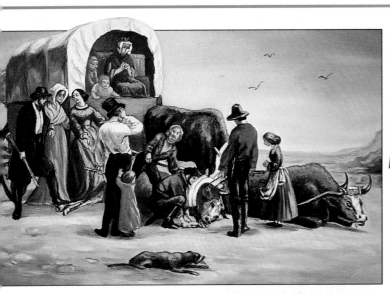

▲ *Panning for gold. Prospectors and miners were among the first settlers to arrive in the West, hoping to make their fortunes.*

▲ *The covered wagon, drawn by oxen, was the usual mode of transport for settlers heading west. As the painting shows, the journey was perilous.*

Buying a state. ▶ *American politicians sign the treaty to buy Alaska from Russia for over $7 million in 1867. It became the 49th state in 1959.*

◀ *Brigham Young was the Mormon leader who led his people to Utah in 1847. They made a new home there and founded Salt Lake City.*

▲ *From sea to shining sea. The first steamer passes through the Panama Canal in 1914, shortening the journey between the Atlantic and the Pacific.*

◀ *Mount St. Helens, Washington, left an area of devastation after it erupted dramatically in 1980.*

1893 Revolution in Hawaii. The islanders establish a republic in 1894

1896 Utah becomes the 45th state

1906 San Francisco destroyed by an earthquake and subsequent fire

1912 Arizona becomes the 48th state. Congress establishes the Alaska Territory

1914 Opening of the Panama Canal aids development of the Pacific rim (construction began in 1904)

1923 The Alaskan Railroad is completed

1931 Gambling is legalized in Nevada and Arizona

1936 The Boulder (Hoover) Dam on the Colorado River is completed

1941 Japan attacks Pearl Harbor, Hawaii, catapulting the United States into World War II

1942 Completion of the Grand Coulee Dam, Washington

1947 Chuck Yeager, flying a Bell X-1 aircraft, becomes the first man to break the sound barrier above Muroc, California

1948 Arizona Native Americans are enfranchised. The 200-inch telescope at Mount Palomar, California, is opened

1959 Alaska becomes the 49th state; Hawaii, the 50th

1963 The Supreme Court settles a 40-year-long dispute and regulates the amount of water to be drawn from the Colorado River by Arizona, Nevada, and California

1980 Mount St. Helens erupts in Washington. Former governor of California Ronald Reagan is elected president

1981 First flight of space shuttle *Columbia* ends safely when it lands at Edwards Air Force Base after spending two days in orbit

1989 Oil spill from the *Exxon Valdez* causes grave environmental damage along the coast of Alaska

Natural Wonders

The western and Pacific region of the United States contains the world's greatest grouping of natural wonders. They range from the Grand Canyon to the black sand beaches of Hawaii, and from Mount McKinley in Alaska to the San Andreas Fault, which runs parallel to the coast and threatens to turn western California into an island one day. The subterranean activity in this region is not new. Crater Lake, near Medford in Oregon, was formed when the top of a volcano was blown off by a prehistoric explosion. The lake, which at 2,000 feet is the second deepest in North America, is 6,177 feet above sea level. There is no apparent outlet for its icy waters.

The Grand Canyon is possibly the best-known natural wonder in the world. It is a 217-mile-long chasm over a mile deep, carved out by the Colorado River and etched by the winds over tens of thousands of years. There are spectacular views from the south rim and from light aircraft that fly into the canyon.

▼ People with vivid imaginations have pictured the cliffs of Bryce Canyon as resembling "soldiers in Turkish pantaloons"—or even clouds.

▲ Dwarfing even the giant sequoia trees, the peaks of Yosemite National Park, California, rear up in splendor along the skyline.

Death Valley, in California, is a long-dried lake that now contains one of the world's loneliest roads. Temperatures there are extremely high during the summer, and solo travelers really do risk losing their lives. More welcoming are the many national parks in this region. Bryce Canyon National Park, in Utah, is a spectacular example. Its pink cliffs and gorges have been carved into remarkable shapes by wind and water over eons of time. Yosemite National Park in the Sierra Nevada is mostly a region of weathered granite towers. But the scenery is enlivened by a variety of lakes, streams, and waterfalls. The park is home to giant sequoias, or redwood trees, which are unique to the region.

▼ *An awe-inspiring view of the Grand Canyon. It is so deep that the climate changes significantly as you make your way down.*

Black volcanic sand is ▶ *strewn across Kalapana Beach on Hawaii Island, making the rolling Pacific surf look even whiter by contrast.*

▲ *New life is now springing up on the slopes of Mount St. Helens after its eruption in 1980. It is seen here across the waters of Spirit Lake.*

Flora and Fauna

This is a region that includes a vast array of climates and conditions—from the dry deserts of Nevada and the tropics of Hawaii to the arctic glaciers of Alaska. So it is not surprising to find a wide variety of plant and animal life there, too.

The deserts boast many types of cactus and other plants. These include the saguaro, the largest American cactus, which grows up to 50 feet high and plays host to owls and other birds. Desert animals include the coyote, the wild javelina pig, and the Gila monster—a large, poisonous lizard.

Up in Alaska, seabirds proliferate—although coastal areas farther south boast the huge California condor. And the Hawaiian Islands have an ecology all their own, with such regional specialties as the mokihana berry, the wahoo fish, and the Hawaiian honey creeper, the most famous of Hawaiian birds.

▲ *This stumpy-tailed desert dweller packs a mean bite. The Gila monster's venom is secreted in grooves in its lower jaw. It can be lethal.*

◀ *Grizzly by name, grumpy by nature, this huge bear gets its name from the speckling of white hairs in its brown coat. Its razorlike claws are used to dig out ground squirrels, which, along with salmon and other small creatures, make up its diet.*

Giants of the forest: a ▶ stately grove of tall redwoods. Many are so big that roads can be bored through their trunks. Some of the largest trees are named after Civil War heroes, like General Sherman and General Grant. But redwood seeds are tiny—123,000 weigh only one pound.

The most dangerous animal in North America, the Far West's grizzly bear stands eight feet tall when it rears up on its hind legs, and weighs 800 to 1,500 pounds. It is very quick-tempered. Another American brown bear is the Alaskan kodiak. It can weigh as much as 1,800 pounds.

The Far West has its share of big trees, too. The redwoods are the tallest trees in the world, reaching up to 275 feet in coastal areas. The tallest of these, in California, is a massive 368 feet high.

Other inhabitants of the region are the tiny kangaroo mouse, the huge ponderosa pine, the creosote bush, the musk-ox, and the deadly little coral snake, which looks dangerously like a discarded necklace. And then there's the Far West's most famous citizen. Chosen in 1782 as the symbol of the United States, the bald eagle is not bald at all—although its white head is deceiving from a distance. It makes its aeries on treetops near the water.

▲ Crowned in spring with wreaths of flowers that only live for one day, the saguaro cactus lives for centuries. Its fruits make delicious jelly.

▼ Noble bird—but a thief. As well as scooping up fish from the water while in flight, the bald eagle will also rob other birds of their catches.

The famous people who were born in, or lived their lives in, the far western and Pacific states all seem to have had a touch of glamour about them, even if many of them predated Hollywood. Whatever they did, they did with a flourish—and many of them are still making the headlines.

Brigham Young (1801–87) A New Englander by birth, Brigham Young studied the teachings of Joseph Smith and was baptized into the Mormon church, or the Church of Jesus Christ of Latter-Day Saints, in 1832. But because they advocated polygamy (marriage to more than one person), the Mormons attracted hostility. They were driven out of Ohio to Illinois, and later out of Illinois, too. Young accepted the leadership of the Mormons in 1846 and trekked via Missouri to Utah, where he founded the settlement there that became Salt Lake City.

William Randolph Hearst (1863–1951) The man who founded a newspaper empire also invented the sensational style of newswriting and presentation known as yellow journalism. The son of a San Francisco mining magnate, Hearst was expelled from Harvard over a practical joke. His father gave him the *San Francisco Examiner*, which he transformed into a successful paper. By 1937, he owned 25 national newspapers in America as well as several famous magazines. His priceless art collection is now on display to the public.

Walt Disney (1901–66) The creator of Mickey Mouse, Donald Duck, and a host of other cartoon characters was born in Chicago but moved to Los Angeles in 1923 to be a filmmaker. His first attempts failed, so he turned to drawing cartoons. In 1928, Mickey Mouse was born, appearing in the first sound cartoon, *Steamboat Willie*. Disney's first full-length animated film, *Snow White*, appeared in 1937. After making films for the government during World War II, Disney turned to "live" subjects like *The Living Desert* (1953) in his later career.

Marilyn Monroe (1926–62) Norma Jean Baker was born in Los Angeles. She was a model for pinup photographs before making her film debut in 1948. She starred in 30 films, mixing drama with comedy. Her beauty, coupled with her apparent naïveté, won her international fame as a sex symbol. But her private life was interwoven with scandal and tragedy, and she died from an overdose of sleeping pills when only 36.

◀ *Headline maker William Randolph Hearst founded a newspaper empire and invented yellow journalism.*

▲ *Cartoon character. When Walt Disney was unable to get into filmmaking, he turned to cartoons and invented Mickey Mouse.*

◀ *Perhaps the most talked-about of all Hollywood film stars is Marilyn Monroe. But her professional success disguised a tragic private life.*

Child star Shirley Temple ▶ (1928–) was a screen sensation in the 1930s. She retired from films at age 21 and later became a United Nations diplomat.

◀ *San Francisco writer Jack London (1876–1916) specialized in stories of the wilderness, wildlife, and men against the elements. His most famous book was The Call of the Wild (1903).*

Californian General George ▶ Patton (1885–1945) earned the nickname Old Blood and Guts for his dramatic military career during World War II.

Sacajawea (c. 1786–1812) Native American woman guide on the Lewis and Clark Expedition, which explored the Far West in 1805–6. Sacajawea obtained the horses needed to cross the Rockies and reach the West Coast.

Cochise (c. 1812–74) Native American leader who waged war against the U.S. Army after relatives of his were hanged by U.S. soldiers for a crime they did not commit. He was known for his courage, integrity, and military skill.

King Kamehameha I (c. 1758–1819) The Hawaiian leader who used his tactical ability and diplomatic skills to bring together the various warring tribes on the islands, uniting the kingdom for the first time.

Sam Goldwyn (1882–1974) A Polish immigrant who settled in Hollywood and became a leading filmmaker and talent spotter.

Mel Blanc (1908–89) Oregonian Blanc was the voice of some of the most famous cartoon characters of all time— including Bugs Bunny.

Richard M. Nixon (1913–) Born in Yorba Linda, California, he served as vice president before becoming president in 1969. He resigned in 1974 over the Watergate scandal.

Sandra Day O'Connor (1930–) Born in Arizona, she became the first woman to sit on the Supreme Court when appointed by Ronald Reagan in 1981.

The Great Cities

San Francisco, California, spreads over a series of hills, many of which offer beautiful views of San Francisco Bay and the Golden Gate Bridge. A major Pacific port and financial and insurance center, this cosmopolitan city is also a cultural, tourist, and shopping mecca.

Anchorage Alaska's largest and most modern city, Anchorage is also at the crossroads of the world's polar aviation routes. Hemmed in by mountains on three sides, the city was founded as a railroad construction camp. It has based its wealth on oil but retains its links with both its Native American and Eskimo cultures. From Earthquake Park, there are grand views of 20,320-foot Mount McKinley, the nation's highest peak.

Honolulu The capital of Hawaii, it sprawls along the coast of the island of Oahu. It boasts luxurious beachfront hotels, lovely views, and fine shopping. The mild year-round climate makes it a sporting paradise.

▲ *Clocks are banned in Las Vegas, Nevada, where neon lights turn night into day. First-class entertainment and gambling make this a top resort.*

High-rise buildings and ▶ busy freeways are the hallmark of downtown Los Angeles. But in its entirety, the "Big Orange" covers a vast metropolitan area.

One of the world's most ▶ famous stretches of shoreline is the seafront of Honolulu, capital of the Hawaiian Islands, where hotels seem to jostle one another for space.

▼ *Alaskan snowscape. The 1st National Bank building in Anchorage, the largest and most modern city in Alaska, attempts to outshine the soaring Chugach Mountains.*

▲ *Sunburst fountain in the Valley of the Sun: the Civic Center fountain and Valley Bank building in Phoenix, Arizona*

▼ *The roads plunge steeply downhill while many of the buildings soar giddily skyward. San Francisco is one of the world's most beautiful cities.*

Las Vegas A man-made desert oasis of endless neon lights and round-the-clock activity, Las Vegas, Nevada, can justly claim to be the entertainment capital of the world. Besides gambling, the hotels and casinos offer shows featuring some of the best-known names in entertainment.

Los Angeles, California, does not have much of a city center. In tourism terms, its outer edges are somewhat blurred, too. That's because many of southern California's vacation stops, like Disneyland, are in outlying areas rather than in Los Angeles itself. Downtown Los Angeles does boast a very good art museum and a growing number of cultural attractions. But most visitors will also want to head to famous coastal areas like Marina del Rey or inland to Hollywood.

Phoenix At the heart of the Valley of the Sun, Phoenix, Arizona, with its satellite suburbs, is one of the fastest-growing cities in America. A desert area greened by irrigation and with spiny cacti rather than trees shading the streets, Phoenix has an agreeably dry climate.

Further Reading about the Fifty States

Brandt, Sue R. *Facts about the Fifty States*. New York: Franklin Watts, 1988.

Collins, Richard, ed. *The Native Americans*. New York: Smithmark Publishers Inc., 1991.

Gildart, Robert, and James Murfin. *The United States of America*. New York: Gallery Books, 1986.

Mathes, Charles. *The Spirit of America: A State-by-State Celebration*. New York: Gallery Books, 1990.

Nevins, Allan, and Henry Steele Commager. *A Short History of the United States*. 6th ed. New York: Alfred A. Knopf, 1984.

Shapiro, William E., ed. *The Young People's Encyclopedia of the United States*. 3 vols. Brookfield, Conn.: The Millbrook Press, Inc., 1992.

Wenborn, Neil. *The U.S.A: A Chronicle in Pictures*. New York: Smithmark Publishers Inc., 1991.

Picture Credits

The publishers would like to thank the picture agencies and photographers who supplied the photographs reproduced in this book. Pictures are credited by page numbers.

The Bettmann Archive: 4, 6–7, 12, 13 upper, 17 top, 18, 19 top, 19 top, middle, and lower left, 24, 25 upper and lower left, 29 top, 30–31, 36, 37 top left, middle left, and lower left, 40, 42, 42–43, 43 upper and middle, 48, 49 lower right, 52, 54, 55 (top left and right, middle, and lower left), 60, 61 upper left. **FPG International:** title page, 2–3 (S. Gottlieb), 5 lower left (Bill Losh), 13 (four lower pictures), 14 left (David Noble), 14 right (James Blank), 14–15 (David Noble), 15 upper left (Dennis Hallinan), 15 upper right (Peter Gridley), 17 lower right (John Scowen), 22 right (Gary Randall), 25 middle left and lower right, 26 lower left (James Blank), 26 lower right (Joachim Messerschmidt), 26–27 (Telegraph Colour Library), 27 upper (Peter Gridley), 27 lower (Terry Qing), 29 middle, 32 lower (Joe Crachiola), 33 lower (Dick Dietrich), 34–35 (Neal Weisenberg), 37 top right and middle right, 38 lower left (James Blank), 38 upper right (H. G. Ross), 38–39 (James Blank), 39 upper left (Travelpix), 41 upper (John Scowen), 41 lower left (E. Nagele), 43 lower (David Bartruff), 44 lower left (Dick Dietrich), 45 upper (Stan Osolinski), 49 upper left, 49 lower left, 50 (Travelpix), 50–51 upper (David Noble), 50–51 lower (James Blank), 51 upper and middle (James Blank), 53 top (Otto Eberhard), 53 lower left (Galen Rowell), 53 lower right (James Blank), 55 lower right (D. C. Lowe), 56 upper (Travelpix), 56 lower (E. Nagele), 57 upper (Dennis Hallinan), 57 lower left (Dick Dietrich), 58 lower (L. Rue), 58–59 (G. Schwartz), 59 lower right (Lee Kuhn), 61 upper right, middle, and bottom, 62 upper (J. Messerschmidt), 62 lower right (Travelpix), 63 lower right (D. C. Lowe). **Frank**

Lane Picture Agency: 10 upper left (A. J. Roberts), 10 upper right (Leonard Lee Rue), 10 lower (S. McCutcheon), 11 upper (Ron Austing), 11 lower left (B. Borrell Casals), 11 lower right (M. B. Withers), 23 upper (Fritz Pölking), 46–47 (L. Lee Rue), 58 upper (Evan Davis). **NASA:** 19 lower right. **Photo Researchers, Inc.:** 2 (Earl Scott), 5 upper (Hal Kinsler), 5 lower right (Blair Seitz), 8 upper (Jerry Cooke), 8 lower (G. H. Kirkpatrick), 9 upper left (Anne LaBastille), 9 upper right (Jerome Wexler), 9 lower (Jack Dermid), 17 lower left (Dale Boyer), 17 middle (M. and S. Landre), 20 upper (John Serrao), 20 lower (Leonard Lee Rue IV), 21 top (John Buitenkant), 21 middle (Thomas England), 21 lower (James R. Fisher), 22 lower left (Norm Thomas), 23 lower left (W. Munoz), 23 lower right (M. P. Kahl), 28–29 (Garry McMichael), 32 upper (Irvin Oakes), 33 upper (L. West), 34 upper (Leonard Lee Rue III), 34 lower (A. Wharton), 35 upper (M. P. Gadomski), 35 lower (Thomas Martin), 39 upper right (W. D. McIntyre), 41 lower right (Guy Higbee), 44 upper (Norris Taylor), 44–45 (Pat and Tom Leeson), 45 lower left (Daniel Zirinsky), 45 lower right (Harold Hoffman), 46 upper (Craig Lorenz), 46 lower (George Jones), 47 upper (G. C. Kelley), 47 lower (Tom McHugh), 57 lower right (Pat and Tom Leeson), 59 top right (L. Migdale), 62 lower left (Joseph Rychetnik), 63 upper left (Ken Biggs), 63 upper right (Guy Gillette).

Cover pictures: FPG International/D. C. Lowe (front upper left); FPG International/Bill Losh (front upper right); FPG International/James Blank (front bottom middle); Photo Researchers, Inc./Lawrence Migdale (front bottom left); Frank Lane Picture Agency/Fritz Pölking (front bottom right); Eric and David Hosking (back).

Index